A

TALE OF THE TIMES.

BY
THE AUTHOR OF A GOSSIP'S STORY.

DEDICATED BY PERMISSION TO MRS. CARTER.

IN THREE VOLUMES.

VOL. II.

Nor shall the pile of hope God's mercy rear'd,
By vain philosophy be e'er destroy'd:
Eternity, by all or wish'd or fear'd,
Shall be by all or suffer'd or enjoy'd.
MASON's *Elegy on the Death of Lady Coventry.*

THE SECOND EDITION.

LONDON:
PRINTED FOR T. N. LONGMAN AND O. REES,
PATERNOSTER-ROW.
1799.

Printing Statement:

Due to the very old age and scarcity of this book,
many of the pages may be hard to read due to the
blurring of the original text, possible missing pages,
missing text, dark backgrounds and other issues
beyond our control.

Because this is such an important and rare work, we
believe it is best to reproduce this book regardless of
its original condition.

Thank you for your understanding.

A

TALE OF THE TIMES.

CHAP. XVIII.

O how canſt thou renounce the boundleſs ſtore
  Of charms which Nature to her vot'ry yields !
The warbling woodland, the reſounding ſhore,
  The pomp of groves, and garniture of fields;
. All that the genial ray of morning gilds,
And all that echoes to the ſong of even,
 ' All that the mountain's ſheltering boſom ſhields,
And all the dread magnificence of heaven,
O how canſt thou renounce, and hope to be forgiven,
                              BEATTIE.

THE intereſt which the appearance and behaviour of Mr. Powerſcourt had excited in lord Monteith's mind had more permanence than the ſudden emotions to which his diſpoſition was ſubject commonly poſſeſſed. His evaneſcent im-

pulſes

pulſes might generally be compared to the impreſſion which a ſtone makes upon the clear ſurface of a glaſſy lake, which, after having formed a few tremulous circles, ſoon reſumes its natural tranquillity.   But on the preſent occaſion he thought of his good-tempered rival, as he termed him, during moſt part of his journey to Scotland; and, as neither a whiſtle nor a ſong would always excite new ideas, he frequently expreſſed himſelf anxious to know whether the poor fellow had ſhot himſelf: "Yet I proteſt, "my dear Geraldine," he added, "I " do not laugh at him; for, upon my " ſoul, if I were as miſerable as he " ſeems to be, I ſhould think of nothing " but driving out Cupid's arrows with " a brace of bullets."

As lady Monteith's endeavours to divert her lord from ſuſpecting Mr. Powerſcourt's attachment had proved in-

ineffectual, she determined, by that full confidence which Mrs. Evans had recommended, to remove every subject of self-condemnation from her own heart. After having bound his honour by a promise of secrefy, she delivered to him the letters with which I concluded the last Chapter; and she entreated him, as the affair was too serious for levity, to avoid the distressing subject in their future conversations.

Lord Monteith was a stranger to that " green-eyed monster which mocks the meat it feeds on." The preference his lady had recently given him was too avowed, and her conduct, as well as her principles, too correct to raise suspicion even in the heart of a Leontes. On the contrary, Mr. Powerscourt's behaviour excited his warm esteem; and his frank open disposition compelled him to exclaim, " I cannot think, Geraldine, why

B 2 " you

" you preferred me to that noble fellow;
" I hope he will live to come back to
" England, that I may thank him for
" giving me happiness at the expence of
" his own repose.   Let me tell you,
" very few young fellows of my ac-
" quaintance would have acted as he
" has done."

" I hope," said the countess, while
heart-felt pleasure lighted up all the
charms of her intelligent face, " that I
" shall have the satisfaction of present-
" ing two friends to each other, highly
" deserving of mutual confidence.   You
" see I have requested Henry's corre-
" spondence; you, my lord, must permit
" me to communicate it to you; your
" superior knowledge of the character of
" your own sex will enable me to discover
" whether his travels are conducive
" to his repose; and you will assist my
" replies by pointing out such topics as
" will

" will prove moſt effectual in promoting
" this end, ever remembering that the
" eſteem and gratitude I now feel for him
" muſt be ſubſervient to the ſtronger at-
" tachment whence they originated."

Such were the ſentiments of lady
Monteith; and ſuch is the conduct upon
which the muſe of hiſtory and the muſe
of fiction alike delight to dwell. The
uncorrupted mind avows its divine original, by recurring with ſecret complacency to the portrait of what is perfect,
fair, and good. Though the depravity
of modern manners may obtain tranſient
amuſement from thoſe highly-coloured
ſcenes of guilt which the judgment con-
demns, the ſoul only finds conſtant gratification in contemplating the lovely
pictures of innocence and virtue.

When I recollect that the ſubſequent
events of this hiſtory will lead my narrative through many a painful ſcene, I

ſeem

seem to shrink with reluctance from the
disgusting task of describing systematic
villany mining the outworks which decorum and religion have placed around
female virtue, while the unsuspecting
heart becomes entangled by satanic guile
and inbred vanity. I feel that the part
most analogous to my taste, as well as
to my powers, would be to depicture
the amiable features of the human character shaded only by those lighter traits
of frailty from which the most perfect
standard of human goodness is not exempt. But, knowing that the unchrist-
ian morals of the present age strain their
affected charity till they embrace vice,
while the most glaring enormities are
glossed over by delicate subterfuges; and
refined liberality expatiates on the goodness of the heart, while its possessor
breaks every precept in the decalogue;
I feel stimulated by an ardent, though
                              perhaps

perhaps injudicious zeal, to lend my feeble aid to stop the torrent of enthusiastic sentiment which daringly menaces that heaven-erected edifice that is predicted to survive the wreck of worlds.

Impressed with this idea, I conceive it possible to serve the cause of principle, by showing through what devious unsuspected paths the human heart may be led to error; how easily it may, by youthful indiscretion, be hurried down the steep descent, till, Hazael-like, it sinks into the infamy which it once shuddered to name. Yet, retaining too much native purity to be reconciled to its degraded state, and too much sensibility to stifle reflection, it shrinks from life as from an insupportable burden; and the morning which rose in splendour is clouded by insuperable gloom before it attains its meridian brightness.

B 4

If

If in the execution of this defign the pencil fhould fail, let Candour remember the intention, and excufe the unfkilful painter. Perhaps the imperfect outline may induce fome fuperior genius, more converfant with life and manners, to execute the inftructive fubject with all the glowing energy that its importance requires.

I fhall gratify my own tafte by dwelling a little longer on that part of lady Monteith's hiftory, when, unaffailed and happy, fhe fpread delight and comfort all around her, and her own heart derived an allowable gratification from the confcioufnefs of deferved applaufe. The firft four years of her married life were unembittered by reftlefs anxiety, corroding difappointment, or the ftill keener pangs of felf-accufation. But, left my readers fhould fuppofe that I am now, falfifying my own maxims, I fhall exhibit

hibit a curfory view of that period which, though it did not include any great forrows or marked deviations from rectitude, ftill bore fome fainter marks of the penalty of Adam.

When the young countefs arrived at Monteith, fhe was aftonifhed at the cruel ravages which time and negligence had made in that venerable pile. Its native magnificence, the fublime features of the adjacent fcenery, every fpot of which feemed by fome traditionary anecdote connected with her lord's family, and the attachment which the peafantry, notwithftanding their extreme wretchednefs, expreffed for the defcendants of their old mafters, kindled in her mind an agreeable enthufiafm, and fhe rejoiced in a diftinction which feemed capable of uniting her own individual happinefs with the general good. Though fhe continued to think that lady Made-

lina

lina carried her ideas of hereditary confequence to a ridiculous extent, a generous heart would find a fair field to
gratify its noblest paffions in the fupremacy of a wide domain. She feemed
never weary of wandering through the
romantic fcenery. "Here," faid fhe,
as fhe one day refted on the flope of a
green hill, over-hung by a pine-clad
precipice, "I will build a neat little
" village. The houfes fhall all be white;
" there fhall be a garden to each, and a
" refidence in this agreeable fpot fhall
" be the reward conferred upon fuch of
" my lord's tenants as feem to fulfil
" their duties with marked propriety:
" I will frequently vifit them; I will be
" their legiflator, their inftructor, their
" phyfician, and their friend. They
" fhall look up to me with gratitude,
" and my own heart fhall enjoy the pure
" recompence of confcious beneficence."

In

In the improvements which she
planned at the caftle, the fame focial
and benevolent fpirit prevailed, though
here perhaps it received a more worldly
teint from the dangerous approximation
of vanity. "Thefe rooms," faid fhe, "if
" embellifhed in the grand Gothic ftyle,
" will fhame the feeble glitter of mo-
" dern frippery. Every article of fur-
" niture fhall be maffy and fubftantial,
" and convey an idea of general ufeful-
" nefs rather than a felfifh defire of ex-
" hibiting the cold enjoyments of unim-
" parted wealth. My lord's fortune is
" ample; I have made to it a confiderable
" addition: how infinitely fhall I prefer
" fpending it upon this fpot, which has
" a local claim to our preference, to
" fquandering it in the unvarying round
" of a London life! Here, without feel-
" ing the pain of competition, expence
" may be juftified by the motive of em-

B 6   " ploying

" ploying industry and diffusing plea-
" sure. I will cultivate the esteem of
" all my neighbours by the most winning
" attentions. The peculiarities which
" entitle me to pre-eminence shall not
" give them uneasiness, because they
" shall be uniformly exerted for their
" pleasure or amusement. Here, without
" observation or interruption, I may
" pursue my plan of influencing lord
" Monteith's taste, till it gradually assi-
" milates to my own. Lady Arabella's
" predilection for a London life, and her
" acknowledged influence over her aunt,
" prevent me from fearing that my
" schemes will be frustrated by the pre-
" sence of those whom I cannot propi-
" tiate and wish not to offend; Distance
" may, perhaps, disarm their prejudices;
" and when personal competition is re-
" moved, the representative of their fa-
" mily may receive those commenda-

" tions

" tions to which kindred or friendſhip
" never can aſpire."

The plans of lady Monteith would
have proved abortive, had ſhe not been
aſſiſted by two powerful coadjutors.
Lord Monteith's natural diſpoſition was
violently diſpoſed to the purſuit of rural
ſports and athletic exerciſes. The
mountains, lakes, and foreſts which
ſurrounded his caſtle, promiſed the
diverſions of fiſhing and hunting in full
perfection; and the neighbouring gentry
had endeavoured to enliven a thinly-
inhabited country by the eſtabliſhment of
an aſſembly, a bowling meeting, and a
cricket match, which returned at ſtated
intervals. The Monteiths honoured
the firſt-mentioned amuſement with
their preſence very ſoon after their
arrival at the caſtle; and, though the
company exhibited but a miniature
reſemblance to the circles in which they
had

had lately moved, they both received
pleasure from the events of the evening.
Two circumstances contributed to his
lordship's satisfaction; he felt himself
perfectly at ease; and, moreover, he
received information, that the neighbouring country afforded what is termed
a set of very hearty fellows, and the
finest grouse and black game in the
kingdom. His pleasure at this intelligence was so great, that while they returned home, he interrupted his lady's
observations on the female part of the
company, by declaring, that since he
found things so agreeable, he really believed he should spend a good deal of time
at Monteith. "I think, Geraldine," said
he, "I cannot be very dull. What do
"you think? I shall hunt one day, fish
"another, go to the bowling-green a
"third; then there will be a cricket
"match, and shooting, and public
                              "dinners,

"dinners, and private parties; and then
"going to Edinburgh if any particu-
"lar bufinefs is on foot, and making
"excurfions through the neighbouring
"counties. I declare I begin to think
"as your father does, that it will be a
"very rational life, and quite as agree-
"able as fpending all our time in thofe
"ftate-trappings of which Arabella is
"fo fond.   She faid that I fhould deteft
"Scotland in a month; but I will con-
"vince her that I can be happy any-
"where.   Don't you think fo too, my
"love? You will like to live here,
"fhall you not?"

"O! infinitely, I affure you; I was
"both furprized and pleafed with the
"manners of feveral of the ladies whom
"I met at the affembly. They feemed
"indeed a little confufed and referved
"at firft, and certainly they are un-
"acquainted with the more refined
                              "modi-

" modifications of politeneſs ; but many
" of them appeared well-informed; and
" I know they will improve upon ac-
" quaintance. I have projected a
" thouſand little ſchemes to inſpire con-
" fidence and cordiality. I am ſure the
" dear old caſtle may ſoon be made
" perfectly comfortable ; and I hope,
" my lord, our reſidence among your
" tenants and dependants will prove an
" eſſential benefit to them."

" I ſhall, certainly, order my ſteward
" to give them the preference upon
" every occaſion which promiſes a
" lucrative advantage."

" Is it impoſſible for us to extend
" our utility further ? Could I not en-
" dow a ſchool, and introduce ſome
" branch of manufacture to employ the
" children and the women ? I am told
" that they are extremely uninformed,
" and in ſome reſpects uncivilized. I

" have

" have fancied that this may be owing
" to the narrow ſtipend of the preſbyter,
" whoſe poverty will not permit him to
" exert that influence over his flock, or
" to pay them that attention which
" the intereſts of morality and religion
" require.   A ſmall addition to his
" ſtipend would not be felt by us, and
" would probably do more for the
" general improvement of manners in
" the neighbourhood than would be
" effected by a much larger expenditure
" any other way.   I ſee, my lord, you
" ſmile ; but allow me as well as your-
" ſelf to quote my father's authority.
" He has frequently obſerved, that by
" enlarging Mr. Evans's ſphere of uſe-
" fulneſs, he did an act of public bene-
" ficence.   ' I only thought,' he uſed to
" ſay, ' of making one worthy man
" happy ; but ſince Mr. Evans has been
                                " relieved

" relieved from the preffure of want, he
" has made many men happy, aye and
" worthy too.'

" Why there may be fomething in
" what fir William obferves, provided
" one could but be fure of having an
" Evans to deal with. But I fhall have
" no leifure for fchemes of this kind;
" fo you may amufe yourfelf with them
" when you have no other employment.
" You may fet up fchools, portion off
" young girls, and enrich old divines:
" But, remember, no manufactories
" in my neighbourhood.—All our fa-
" mily hate the very name of them.—
" They only encourage a horde of idle
" infolent vagrants, who fly in your face
" upon every occafion."—

" Not if care be taken to improve
" their morals in proportion to their
" affluence. You fee how thinly your
                                    " villages

" villages are peopled, and what ex-
" treme poverty the general appearance
" of the country befpeaks."

" It will be very different when I
" fpend my fortune among them. The
" repairs of the caftle will employ the
" men."

" But the women and children ?"

" O they fhall be fed at the caftle
" gate."

" No; let them eat the bread of in-
" duftry, and enjoy thofe delights
" which the active exertion of our
" native energies always infpires.
" Sweet is the food which is earned
" by labour. When you, my lord,
" purfue health and pleafure in the
" fields and woods, and return home to
" tafte the repofe which is procured by
" exertion, and to partake of the dain-
" ties for which you are indebted to
" your own toil, you feel this maxim
                                " true;

" true; and your heart will exult at the
" idea that your provident benevolence
" has extended fimilar enjoyments to
" hundreds, who muft long need the
" protecting care of their benefac-
" tor, and confequently cannot affect
" an infolent independence on his
" bounty."

Perhaps lord Monteith's principal
objections to his lady's fchemes were,
that he fhould be involved in fome
trouble by the execution of them. Her
judicious allufion to his favourite purfuits in the preceding fpeech, and the
profpect of the honour being wholly
his, while he determined that the dif-
ficulties fhould be exclufively hers;
thefe reafons, added to fome fecret
ideas that if the plan anfwered it would
be another triumph over the prejudices
of his obftinate aunt, procured his acquiefcence, and he uttered the words,
" You

" You fhall do as you pleafe, only don't " teaze me about it," juft as the chariot paffed over the draw-bridge which led to the caftle.

CHAP. XIX.

Say, fhould the philofophic mind difdain
That good which makes each humble bofom vain ?
Let fchool-taught pride diffemble all it can,
Thefe little things are great to little man ;
And wifer he, whofe fympathetic mind
Exults in all the good of all mankind.

GOLDSMITH.

THE *fang froid* with which lord Monteith always treated every fcheme not
immediately connected with his own
pleafures, frequently communicated a
fevere pang to the liberal mind of the
countefs. Her delicacy was hurt at the
grofs character of his amufements, and
her vanity was piqued by perceiving
that the tenacioufnefs of long indulged
habit would not yield to the fafcination
of her refined accomplifhments. Like
Defdemona, fhe was " an excellent
mufician, and could fing the favage-
nefs

ness out of a bear." Her mellifluous
voice and sweet-toned harp still retained
all their exquisite power of transfusing
harmony and delight into her husband's
soul, while the early horn or the convi-
vial appointment called him from the
syren in vain. But if she sought to
lead his attention to the blooming wil-
derness of sweets planted by her hand, or
the scarcely less glowing garland created
by her pencil, he instantly recollected
some insurmountable engagement which
required every moment of his time. She
was equally unfortunate if she attempted
to interest him in the history of her
colony, as she termed her neat little
white village; or if, opening the stores
of her capacious mind, she sought to
discuss some topic of literary taste, her
arguments might be brilliant, but un-
less they were compressed within the
strictest rules of Spartan brevity, her
lord

lord was either difcovering the wit of his fpaniel, or had fallen faft afleep.

Yet his heart was juft to her merits, and his tongue fo copious in her praife; that he was fometimes inclined to thruft in the agreeable fubject without proper preparation. He was confidered by all who vifited at the caftle to be a moft perfect paragon of connubial merit; and lady Monteith was as univerfally pronounced to be a happy woman, with which opinion I am inclined to coincide, notwithftanding that the power of Gyges' magic ring, invariably poffeffed by all novel writers, has enabled me to peep behind the curtain, and to fee the corroding forrow which a prudent wife will not only conceal from public obfervation, but even withhold from the knowledge of her bofom friend.

My young female readers, whofe notions of nuptial felicity are drawn from the

the delufive pages of a circulating
library, will ftart at the harfh tenet
which feems to affirm, that a great
number of married ladies may affign
caufes for difcontent of a feverer nature than what fometimes affected the
tranquillity of the blooming Geraldine.
Fearful left they fhould fuppofe my
doctrine ambiguous, or imagine that the
happinefs of the lady was wholly owing
to the amiable conftitution of her own
mind, I will very plainly tell them,
that, though caufes for vexation occafionally occurred, lafting unhappinefs in
fuch a fituation could only proceed from
a difcontented, ill-regulated temper, or
a perverted judgment, which, inftead
of forming an eftimate of life as it really
is, erects a fallacious ftandard, by which
it decides upon what is due to its own
deferts, and how far others act as they
ought. Reverfe this laft fentence, and

let the fair fcrutinizer of her hufband's faults contemplate the errors of her own behaviour; let her recollect the duties fhe has heedlefsly omitted, and the provocations fhe has undefignedly given; and let her then ufe the experience fhe derives from felf-examination in her eftimate of the conduct of her partner. After making fome deductions, for the ftronger temptations to which the other fex are expofed by their more impetuous paffions and blunter feelings, that indulgence of their humours which their manners in early youth permit, and their hereditary notions of fuperiority derived from Adam; I fay, fhe will then, perhaps, juftly refer the apparent neglect or cruel unkindnefs which had juft extorted her tears, to fomething of bufinefs, which " had puddled his clear temper," and fent him home rather with an expectation of having his

humours

humours foothed by feminine foftnefs, than of offering at the fhrine of feminine fufceptibility thofe attentions which fit the bridal ftate.

The fenfibility of lady Monteith's difpofition prevented her from viewing the defects in her lord with the indifference which a mind of common refinement would have experinced. But to the qualities of refinement and fenfibility, fo generally fatal to female peace, Geraldine united a ftrong attachment to her hufband, natural fweetnefs of temper, and correct notions of the human character, derived from her early intimacy with Mrs. Evans. The precepts of that excellent monitrefs, now ftrengthened by conviction of their propriety, frequently recurred to her mind, prevented her from adopting the language of complaint, opened her eyes to the agreeable part of her fituation,

and

and transferred her attention to what
her own duty required from her, till
native complacency and habitual affection reftored all the fprightly energies
of her mind.

Under her prefiding influence Monteith caftle realized to the idea of every
beholder the delightful vifion of Spen-
fer's Bower of Blifs, governed by a
Una inftead of an Acrafia. Magnificence was united with urbanity, hofpi-
tality was gilded by elegance, while the
prefiding enchantrefs foftened her envi-
able fuperiority in beauty, wealth, wit,
and talents, by the moft unaffecting
condefcenfion, and amiable attention to
the accommodation of her guefts. If her
tafte in drawing extorted admiration
from thofe young ladies who were juft
trying to acquire the rudiments of the
fcience, the pain of that fentiment was
immediately foftened by her ready offer

of

of furnishing them with crayons, pencils,
subjects to copy superior to what the
country afforded, or assistance from the
master who occasionally attended her.
Her tuneful voice and magic touch
could not be imparted; but she had
songs and music books at every one's
service, and she was very willing to
assist in affording all the mechanical aid
which that enchanting science admits.
She had acquired a knowledge of all
fashionable works, and here again in-
struction and materials only waited to
be required. Her library, her conser-
vatory, and her hot-house attracted
general attention, and transfused general
pleasure, because their respective trea-
sures were not kept merely to gratify
the ostentation of the possessor, but
were permitted to impart their mental
riches and odoriferous sweets to any
who wished to read a book or cultivate

an

an off-set. Adhering to the rule, that beauty is best attired when robed by simple elegance, she had no temptation to be guilty of the temerity of attracting envy by the splendour of her ornaments; and the expence spared from her own dress was employed in judicious presents to those of her young friends whose circumstances would ill support the cost of genteel appearance. To crown this fair assemblage of complacent graces, her exquisitely playful wit, while it dazzled by its brilliancy, prevented by its inoffensive sweetness the most irritable mind from charging it with sarcastic severity.

Her village flourished. She had named it James-town, in honour of her lord, to whose liberality she properly referred every improvement of which she was the directing soul. The neighbouring peasantry were emulous

to

to become inhabitants of a fpot which poffeffed fo many local advantages; and a fpirit of order and improvement was gradually introduced. The melancholy highlander no longer watched his few ftarved fheep on the bleak mountain, and for want of occupation foothed his forrows with a bagpipe. One of his younger boys performed that office, while "he earned bread for his infants and health for himfelf," in fhaping the green allies of Monteith, covering the bleak mountains with plantations of Scotch pine and American oak, or digging the foundations of the new buildings, which were continually added to James-town. Befide a neat edifice appropriated to divine worfhip, it poffeffed a carpet manufactory, a fpinning-room, a village fchool, and a market-houfe. Perfons properly qualified were placed at the head of each inftitution, and the

c 4   tafte

tafte of the boys was to be confulted in
their future deftination, while the occupations of fifhing, agriculture, and
weaving, folicited their choice. The views
of the girls were more circumfcribed;
but by being early taught the occupations
of fpinning and knitting, and by having
a market opened for the fale of their
productions, they were relieved from the
burden of indolence, and the cheer-
lefs profpect of being a ufelefs weight
upon their future hufbands, or de-
pendent upon their caprice for every
article of fupport. It was lady Monteith's favourite amufement to take a
morning excurfion to James-town, and
to introduce her female vifitants to the
young feminary which flourifhed under
her care; and it frequently happened,
that fome yellow-haired laffie difplayed
fufficient abilities to induce one of the
countefs's guefts to transfer her from the

tafk

taſk of ſinging at her wheel, to the en-
viable employment of clear-ſtarching
the lady's "kerchiefs;" and helping
" to buſkin her."

Yet even the exertions of liberal benevolence will not always afford a pure
delight; the mind muſt ſeek its ſureſt
reward in the conſcious diſcharge of
an acknowledged duty, and not in the
perfect gratitude nor the complete ſatiſ-
faction of the objects it labours to benefit. Though the inhabitants of James-
town were ſelected from the moſt de-
ſerving part of lord Monteith's tenants,
it does not follow that they were quite
exempt from the failings of humanity.
The houſes were all neat and comfortable; but as the counteſs had amuſed
herſelf by conſtructing them after various models, it might happen that dame
Brown would think gaffer Campbell's
the more convenient, while the gaffer

c 5   for

for a fimilar reafon preferred that inhabited by the dame. Lady Monteith, indeed, confented to their exchanging dwellings; but then another inconvenience arofe; Margery Bruce complained that a window in dame Brown's houfe overlooked her, and that if the faid window was not walled up, fhe could not live; for that the dame took her ftation at that window, and, inftead of minding her work, did nothing but watch the conduct of the aggrieved deponent. Dame Brown's rejoinder was, that Margery was fufpected to be no better than fhe fhould be; that fhe had lately got a new plaid and kirtle, nobody knew how; and fhe thought it her duty to mind her goings on, left her good lady fhould be impofed upon by an unworthy pretender to her favours. The fair judge found it difficult to decide in a queftion of fuch nice morality;

and

and the more fo, as the village was fplit
into two nearly equal factions, part en-
lifting under the banners of the watchful
Brown, and part efpoufing the caufe of
the aggrieved Margery.

Befide the perplexity which cafes fimilar to the above often excited, lady
Monteith had to contend with other inconveniencies. The power of local
attachment is very ftrong in people who
have paffed their lives on one fpot, without having had much intercourfe with
the reft of the world; and fhe often
found that the old Highlander preferred
" the hill that lifted him to the ftorms,"
to all the advantages which, while un-
tried, his imagination annexed to the
fheltered cultivated valley. The manners of the fouthern ftrangers, whom
the ornamental embellifhments of Monteith had introduced among the new
colony, did not affimilate with his pre-

c 6   conceived

conceived ideas of fubmiffion, œconomy, and felf-command. Though invited to partake of the luxuries his new neighbours introduced, his affection for four-crout and crowdy was infurmountable, and his retired folitary humour fhrunk from the loquacious interruptions of fociety. He frequently found that he had renounced pleafures congenial to his habits, for comforts which he wanted the relifh to enjoy; and though refpect for his gude laird and lady checked complaint, the fmothered difcontent often made him meet the inquiries of the latter with the fombrous brow of forrow inftead of the funfhine of joy. "Ye meant it," he would fay, "aw' for "the beeft, but my ain auld cot was "mair cumfurtable."

"Is virtue then only a name?" the contemplative Geraldine would fome-times inquire, when ruminating on the untoward

untoward events which often croffed her
benevolent fchemes. "I have been
"taught to confider the power of be-
"ftowing happinefs as the moft glo-
"rious prerogative which wealth could
"enjoy. Have the means by which I
"purfued this end been ill felected, or
"am I particularly unfucefsful in
"choofing fit fubjects for my defign?"
The philofophy of one-and-twenty is not
remarkably profound; the views of life
are then too highly coloured to admit
of the "yellow leaf," which "fober
autumn" gradually introduces; and the
error then prevalent even in the beft-
regulated minds is, that the fcenes in
which themfelves are actors furnifh
exemptions to received rules as to the
maxims by which they are to be governed, or the forrows and difappoint-
ments which they are to encounter.
Difpaffionate experience would have
taught

taught lady Monteith, that the very circumſtances of the villagers' complaints
argued comparative comfort. Pining
poverty, deep affliction, and hopeleſs
miſery, would have adopted themes for
lamentation widely different from the
ſuperior convenience of gaffer Campbell's
houſe, the impertinence of dame Brown,
the ſuſpicious finery of Margery Bruce,
or even the remembrance of ſour-crout
and crowdy, which haunted the "auld"
Highlander. Her liberal mind would
then have added to the certain ſatisfaction
of a pure intention the exhilarating enjoyment of that moderate ſucceſs to
which all ſublunary ſchemes can alone
aſpire; and ſhe would have judged of
the happineſs of her colony, as one of
our critics has obſerved of the ſorrows
of Paſtoral: " That it is a ſufficient re-
" commendation of any ſtate, when they
" have no greater miſeries to deplore."

A full

A full conviction of that depreſſing but infallible truth, that all the good of this world muſt be blended with evil, would alſo have preſerved lady Monteith from the mortifications to which her love of diſtinction and univerſal applauſe likewiſe expoſed her. Againſt the ſhafts which, in ſpite of repeated obligations, low envy and petty detraction ſometimes aimed at her character, ſweetneſs of temper and conſcious ſuperiority oppoſed an inadequate defence. Lady Monteith's letters to her dear Lucy have contained a gentle complaint againſt ingratitude and the hardſhips of her own lot; for, though anxiouſly ſolicitous to oblige and conciliate her neighbours and acquaintance, ſhe often found her well-meant endeavours miſtaken, or repaid by diſlike and diſcontent.

If

If Miſs Evans did not always feel the
force of her friend's complaints, it muſt
not be aſcribed to the diminution of her
affection, nor to a want of ſympathy.
I have already obſerved, that her mind
was of a ſtronger caſt; it was, beſide,
more intimately acquainted with real
calamity.

CHAP. XX.

When thy laſt breath, ere nature ſunk to reſt,
Thy meek ſubmiſſion to thy God expreſs'd;
When thy laſt look, ere thought and feeling fled,
A mingled gleam of hope and triumph ſhed.
PLEASURES OF MEMORY.

THE reader will remember that I left Mrs. Evans ſtruggling with the violence of a cruel diſeaſe, whoſe reiterated attack ſeemed to leave little hope of the preſervation of her valuable life. She endured her allotted miſeries with exemplary patience, and after her ſufferings had almoſt taught her diſconſolate friends to wiſh for her deliverance, ſhe meekly cloſed a well-ſpent life, bequeathing the invaluable legacy of her virtues to her beloved daughter.

When lady Monteith received the painful tidings, ſhe was in hourly expectation

pectation of her firft confinement; and
the utter impoffibility of taking fuch a
long journey alone prevented her from
exerting her perfonal fervices to footh
her Lucy's forrows. She wrote to her
in the tendereft ftrain of affectionate
condolence. " My tears," faid fhe,
" fhall ever mingle with yours over the
" facred remains of my monitrefs, my
" fofter-mother, my firft and moft va-
" luable friend! Every good action I
" perform, every evil I efcape, every
" commendable fentiment that rifes in
" my heart, is owing to her. Her in-
" valuable precepts, fanctioned by ex-
" perience, now acquire refiftlefs effi-
" cacy from the painful reflection that
" her lips can repeat them no more. I
" brood over them in my memory as a
" facred treafure. Come to me, my
" deareft Lucy; my prefent fituation,
" which excludes ftrangers, demands your
" tender

" tender foothings, and will fuit the pri-
" vacy of your modeft grief. Come, and
" tell me, while it is frefh in your me-
" mory, all that the dying faint faid, all
" that fhe looked ; and arm my fortitude
" for the trials which await me, by repeat-
" ing how fhe endured months of mifery."

" It was the folemn injunction of my
" now bleffed mother," faid Mifs Evans,
in her reply, " that I fhould devote my-
" felf to the pious office of foothing the
" forrows of my poor father, till time,
" uniting with religious refignation,
" fhould foften his griefs, divert his
" thoughts from one painful object, and
" enable him to occupy his leifure hours,
" once fo happily filled, with other
" amufements ; and fhe enjoined this
" duty as the nobleft method of proving
" my affectionate regard for her memory.
" She even added, that fhe hoped her
" dif-

" difembodied fpirit might be permitted
" to witnefs my perfeverance in a mode
" of conduct, the knowledge of which
" would perfect her beatitude.

" Is this the only way by which I can
" now prove my filial reverence to the
" beft of mothers, and fhall I fhrink
" from the important charge? Even
" your claims upon me, my deareft Ge-
" raldine, are annihilated by this fuperior
" tie. You will rejoice to hear that I
" am fuccefsful. My poor father was
" furprized into an agony of grief laft
" Sunday. We attended divine fervice,
" though he could not attempt to per-
" form the duty. The fight of my
" mother's prayer-book lying upon her
" vacant feat overpowered him. His
" ftifled fobs were heard by feveral of
" the congregation; I knelt by his fide,
" I preffed his revered hand to my lips;
" I feemed at that moment to have a
                              " perfect

" perfect control over my own feelings;
" I whifpered, that his only remaining
" Lucy would endeavour to fupply the
" place of her whom Providence had
" removed to a better world. My fa-
" ther viewed me with ferene delight,
" and, as we walked home, he told me
" that I was indeed his comforter, and
" worthy of my excellent mother.

" His praife is a cordial to my heart.
" While fhe lived, I thought my con-
" duct as a daughter not blamable ; but
" now that fhe is beyond the reach of
" my attention, I find infinite occafion
" for felf-reproach. The thought that
" we have paid the laft offices to a be-
" loved object is inconceivably painful.
" It turns the mind to a retrofpective
" view of its paft fentiments ; and the
" remembrance of cafual neglects and
" inadvertent expreffions is torture. If
" thou, my mother ! couldft arife from
" thy

" thy earthy bed, how would thy Lucy
" feek to endear thy renewed exiftence
" by redoubled attentions and more
" fteady virtues! Pardon, thou dear
" faint! my imperfect duty; I muft
" enjoy the thought that thou art pre-
" fent, and confcious of thofe fighs and
" tears which I generally conceal from
" every other eye.

" Do not think, my dear Geraldine,
" that I fhall ever forget the particulars
" of her dying moments. The awful
" remembrance is engraven upon my
" mind, and no fubfequent events can
" obliterate the impreffion. I will de-
" fcribe it all to you when we meet; at
" that time, I truft, both the hearer and
" the relater will be more equal to the
" defcription.

" The exprefs which has juft arrived
" at the manor-houfe relieves my heart
" from many anxieties. You are in
" fafety,

" safety, my Geraldine; you are bleſſed
" with a daughter. Your uſeful life is
" ſpared to your huſband, your infant,
" your father, your friends, your country.
" It is a general, a public benefit: but
" let your dejected Lucy lift her grateful
" voice amid the univerſal joy, and
" adore that kind Providence which has
" preſerved her from further depriva-
" tions.

" We ſhall meet, my beloved friend,
" and I truſt ſoon. Sir William has
" juſt left us. He is in raptures at this
" event, though a little inclined to re-
" gret that he has not a grandſon. It
" is all for the beſt, he ſays; he doubts
" not, when he ſees the pretty creature,
" he ſhall be as fond of it as he was of
" his own Geraldine. ' I took it a little
" hard,' ſaid he, ' that my girl did not
" come to Powerſcourt at the time
" prefixed; but ſhe will now bring the
" dear

" dear infant along with her, and I shall
" have two pleasures instead of one.'

"Excellent man! He has laid a
" scheme, he says, to make us all happy
" together. He insists that my father
" and I shall live with you at the manor-
" house during the time of your ex-
" pected visit. He says, he can divert Mr.
" Evans with a hit at backgammon;
" and that it will do my spirits good to
" have a great deal of chat with you.
" 'Don't be so cast down, my dear god-
" daughter,' he continued, ' we are all
" mortal you know; and your good mo-
" ther is now much happier than it was
" even in your power to make her.'

" I know you love to hear your
" father's words repeated with all their
" genuine benevolence and simplicity.
" He has truly fulfilled the precept of
" frequenting the house of mourning.
" Scarcely a day has passed without his
                              " visiting

" vifiting us, and his kind folicitude
" has been attended with confiderable
" advantage. It is impoffible to con-
" verfe with him without feeling a por-
" tion of his tranquil fpirit diffufed into
" our own bofoms.

" Adieu, dear lady Monteith ! How
" I long to fee, you in your matronly
" character, to fold your little babe in
" my arms, and in the contemplation
" of your deferved felicity to lofe for a
" time the recollection of my own irre-
" mediable forrows !"

Lady Monteith's recovery was rapid,
and fhe was foon able to introduce the
young nurfery to the eager expectants
at Powerfcourt. Her lord, though ex-
ceffively anxious for her fafe journey,
and doatingly fond of his little moppet,
would not accompany them. Bufinefs
of the greateft importance prevented
him; his engagements at fifhing parties,

bowling meetings, and cricket matches, were fo numerous, that it was abfolutely impoffible to break them.   " Take " the greateft care of yourfelf, therefore, " my dear Geraldine, till I can come " and take care of you.   You may de- " pend upon it, that I fhall fet off to " fee your father act ' the old courtier " of the Queen's, the firft moment I am " difengaged, for I cannot long be happy " without you.   By the bye I think " your father unreafonable in infifting " upon having fo much of your com- " pany."

I pafs by fir William's rapturous re- ception of his daughter, the unaffected tranfport of the countefs, and the tears of mingled pain and pleafure which ftole filently down Lucy's faded cheek.   I fhall not dwell upon the unaffected dignity with which Mr. Evans ftrove to prevent his forrows from cafting a gloom

gloom over the general joy, nor the repeated marks of grateful veneration and
affection which lady Monteith paid to
the memory of her deceased friend.
We will suppose that, holding by her
Lucy's arm, she visited the spot which
contained the sacred remains of her lost
monitress; that she listened to the interesting narrative of her sickness and
death, and, mingling her own tears with
those of her amiable companion, repeated the remembered precepts of the
guardian of her youth, and enjoined
upon herself the imitation of her virtues.
The reader will recollect, that to these
duties lady Monteith had added an additional bond,—a promise given to the
deceased, " that if her friendship could
" avail, her Lucy should never be un-
" happy."

It will also be remembered, that Mr.
Powerscourt frequently wrote to his

D 2   cousin,

coufin, and that lord Monteith was invited to overlook the correfpondence.
He fincerely wifhed Henry well; he
would rather not have his wife make
any man miferable; and when he con-
trafted his own character with the refinement and intelligence vifible in his
rival's letters, he felt a little awkward,
and inclined to think that her coufin's
tafte was more congenial to lady Monteith's than his own. All thefe reafons
made him very defirous that Henry
fhould break Cupid's fetters; but fince
he was confident that he was a very
honeft fellow, and that nobody could
doubt his wife's propriety, he was anxious to efcape the trouble of reading
the correfpondence; for Henry's letters
were generally very long, and chiefly
about places which he had vifited in his
travels; befide, lord Monteith was always terribly incommoded by want of
leifure. The countefs was therefore
left

left to her own obfervations, which pointed out to her that Henry's increaf-ing vivacity augured well; and, to con-firm the fatisfaction which his recovered cheerfulnefs diffufed over her mind, his laft letter expreffed an intention of re-turning to England by the route of Lower Germany, Switzerland, and Flanders.

It was the encouraging hope which thefe circumftances fupplied, and not the ftimulation of feminine curiofity, that induced lady Monteith to develope her friend's fentiments in a point that had hitherto been guarded by the moft rigid fecrefy. She endeavoured gra-dually to lead her to the fubject, and began by expatiating on the beauties of Monteith. " My lord," faid fhe, " has " kindly permitted me to indulge a " thoufand little whimfeys in embellifh-" ing a fpot eminently indebted to na-

D 3　　　　　" ture.

" ture. I have fet up temples and al-
" coves out of number. Some are for
" folitary mufings, others for focial
" parties. There is one, of which I
" hope, Lucy, you will be very fond,
" and that we fhall fpend many happy
" hours there, when you come to ftay
" with us next autumn. It is formed
" upon a plan communicated by Henry
" Powerfcourt ; he took it from a beau-
" tiful ruin in Campania. It is open
" to the fouth, and fhaded by the
" loftieft beeches I ever faw. The ivy
" and woodbines which I have planted
" round fome of the columns grow very
" good-humouredly. It has befides
" the advantage of a profpect, to which
" even the mountain fcenery of Powerf-
" court is flat and uninterefting."

A crimfon blufh lighted up Mifs
Evans's face. " It is," faid fhe, " ex-
" tremely doubtful whether the ftate of

" my

" my father's spirits will allow me to
" spend next autumn with you. But
" you mentioned Mr. Powerscourt—
" I hope he is well. When did you
" hear of him ?"

" Very lately," said the countess,
drawing out one of his letters. " He
" writes in excellent spirits, and he
" gives us hopes of his soon returning
" to England. I hope, Lucy, you will
" meet him at Monteith."

" I meet him ?" replied Lucy, in in-
creasing agitation.

" Yes, my love—I am sure you will
" have a sincere pleasure in renewing
" your acquaintance with an old friend.
" In this very letter he expresses a most
" lively concern for your loss, and a
" strong solicitude for your happiness."

" You were always a little inclined
" to fib," replied Lucy, with a smile
which revived the idea of her native

signi-

fignificant archnefs. " It is *your* happi-
" nefs for which he feels fuch ftrong
" folicitude."

" Read then, and be convinced,"
faid the countefs, tendering her the
letter.

" No," faid Lucy, recollecting herfelf, and affuming a ferious air; " I fhall
" preferve the pertinacity afcribed to
" my fex, and refufe conviction till you,
" dear tempter, tell me, what good
" would arife from my indulging a vain
" hope, that I excite an intereft in Mr.
" Powerfcourt's heart. You know my
" fecret, Geraldine; and let me for ever
" filence your obfervations on this fub-
" ject, by owning that I know his. If
" I have not your charms to attract his
" affection, I have at leaft fortitude to
" avoid his contempt. His regret at
" lofing the woman of his choice fhall
" not be aggravated by compaffion for
                              " a love-

" a love-lorn girl, who, betrayed by
" inexperience to unfolicited love, pur-
" fues him with the offer of an unac-
" cepted heart."

" I admire your lovely pride," faid
the countefs. " Yet my friend's deli-
" cacy need not be hurt when I declare,
" that, as nothing but a pre-attachment
" would have made me infenfible to
" Henry's merits, it is my moft earneft
" wifh that fhe may reward them."

" How reward them, lady Monteith?
" Can a forced alliance (and pity is com-
" pulfion to a noble mind) reward the
" generous, firm, felf-denying virtues
" of Harry Powerfcourt? Shall the
" man who could renounce a bleffing
" his whole foul was ardent to poffefs,
" even when by that renunciation he
" expofed himfelf to the anger of the
" friend he beft loved, be linked to a
" woman who found the ties of delicacy

" too

" too weak to reſtrain her ſelfiſh pre-
" ference ?"

" Can a lively ſenſibility of ſuperior
" goodneſs efface the delicacy of your
" character? No, my Lucy, it gives to
" it a more intereſting attraction. Yet
" I perfectly agree with you, that it
" ought to be kept ſecret from the
" object of your regard; for, till Henry
" is juſt to your merits, even he is
" unworthy of you."

" And is he not, in your ſenſe of the
" word, unjuſt ?"

" I own that his heart was beſtowed
" where its value was leſs eſteemed;
" but ſince that attachment is now ut-
" terly at an end——"

" Go on, my ſweet flatterer, and ſay
" in plain terms, Now that I am mar-
" ried, do you, Lucy, come and meet
" the agreeable bachelor at Monteith :
                                    " throw

" throw yourself in his way, study his
" humours, and try to persuade him to
" take a little notice of you.—No,
" Geraldine; the man who has loved
" you will not easily be caught by other
" lures; and, dearly as I regard you, I
" shall be too tenacious of my own
" right of pre-eminence to admit of your
" participation of my husband's heart."

" His return to England," replied
the countess, " is a clear proof that
" he can view me with indifference.
" Must the man who has been un-
" fortunate in his first choice necef-
" sarily remain for ever after infensi-
" ble to female merit? Surely, Lucy,
" that romantic idea was never incul-
" cated by your mother's precepts."

" Such a change is not absolutely
" impossible; but highly improbable
" in the present instance. Observe the
" line of conduct which I mean steadily

" to

" to purfue ; and I conjure you by our
" friendfhip, and your wifhes for my
" happinefs do not attempt to make
" me deviate from it. I. fhall in the
" firft place perfift in my endeavours to
" conquer a preference which promifes
" to be always irreconcilable with my
" peace ; and, as a means to forward this
" defirable end, neither in your letters
" nor your converfation do you, my Ge-
" raldine, introduce the painful theme.
" I will neither avoid nor feek Mr.
" Powerfcourt ; I will neither appear
" anxious to pleafe, nor fearful to offend
" him. Whatever progrefs I make in
" his affections fhall be all in my own
" natural character. Do you exert your
" penetration, and warn me when I de-
" part from this line of conduct. Be
" as jealous of my delicacy as you
" would of your own ; and if ever my
" countenance betrays in his prefence
                                    " the

" the perturbation of my mind, warn
" me of the danger of exciting my own
" future remorfe; and let me haften
" back to hide my folly in this folitude,
" where my mind fhall foon regain its
" loft energy by the contemplation of
" my mother's virtues."

She then prefented lady Monteith
with a copy of verfes. " Read," faid
fhe, " this little tribute to filial duty,
" which burft from my heart during my
" lonely walk laft night. It is not finifh-
" ed, but it will convince you that I am
" capable of more worthy feelings than
" the weak regrets of unrequited love."
So faying, fhe fuddenly left the countefs,
who with mingled admiration and regret
perufed the following fragment:

Still will I wander through thefe mofs-grown
        bowers,
And fcent the grateful fragrance of thefe flowers ;
                                        Still

Still will I pace the paths her footsteps prefs'd,
Still watch the favour'd plants her culture blefs'd;
While the loud throftle warbling fills the grove,
Mix'd with the murmurs of the melting dove.
Here, when the fun's declining car allows
A deeper fhade to hover o'er the boughs,
Sweet Philomel, who fhunn'd the " garifh day,"
Awakes th' enamoured echoes with her lay;
O Bird! beft darling of the Mufe, again
Pour on my penfive ear that thrilling ftrain;
Again repeat it!—Fancy fhall prolong
Thy notes, and give expreffion to thy fong;
Tell what deep fwells defcribe parental woe,
For fever'd love what fofter defcants flow;
Sing on—the tender fympathy I feel,
For, as around me night's dun fhadows fteal,
Keen retrofpection every fenfe employs,
And gives a fubftance to departed joys.
I fee thy form, my honour'd mother! glide
Wrapt in a filmy mift, and fcarce defcried;
I turn delighted, and again rejoice
In the known cadence of thy filver voice.
O! ever-lov'd, rever'd, lamented, fay,
From what far region haft thou wing'd thy way?
Charg'd with what kind injunction art thou come
To turn my footfteps from the path-worn tomb?

Appear'ft

Appear'st thou in difpleafure, to upbraid
Some broken promife, or fome rite unpaid;
Or haft thou journey'd to this dark terrene
To tell the fecrets of the world unfeen?—
'Tis filence all—Light zephyrs wave the trees,—
'Twas but the glancing boughs, and rifing breeze;
The faint impreffion fades upon my brain,
The vifion clofes, but my griefs remain!

CHAP. XXI.

Still to ourfelves in every place confign'd,
Our own felicity we make or find:
With fecret courfe, while no loud ftorms annoy,
Glides the fmooth current of domeftic joy.

GOLDSMITH.

AMONG the various means employed
by Providence to foften human calamity,
none are more eminently beneficial than
the opiates which time adminifters to
grief. It was finely obferved by a
novelift, (not one of the prefent fchool,)
that none but the guilty are long and
completely miferable. In vain does
the foul, while labouring under the
ftrong paroxyfms of calamity or difappointment, renounce all acquaintance
with terreftrial pleafures, and, like the
Hebrew patriarch, refolve to " go down

to

to the grave mourning." Time will
soften the poignancy of regret; a Ben-
jamin may arise to divert affection from
the grave of Joseph, and the tears of
anguish may be converted to those of
joy. This supposition, however, pre-
mises that the grief did not originate in
the depravity of the sufferer. Inter-
vening years may render vice callous or
penitent; but the impenetrability of one
state, and the apprehensiveness of the
other, are alike irreconcilable with the
idea of happiness. It has been long acknowledged, that, though the loss of a
beloved friend seems at first the most
insupportable of all calamities, even
affectionate minds sooner acquiesce in
such deprivations, than they do in many
other kinds of distress. This may
sometimes be accounted for upon religious principles; but even when it
does not own such exalted motives, it
seems

feems fevere to afcribe it to levity of
difpofition. Exifting in the midft of a
dying world, we fhould rather employ
our faculties in extracting improvement
from fcenes of mortality, than wafte
them in unavailing regret. The bond
of friendfhip is not, indeed, diffolved
by death; yet it does not impofe incef-
fant woe on the furvivor, who muft foon
journey through the fame dark valley
which the lamented object has juft explored.

Strengthened by fuch confiderations,
ftill further enforced by the precepts and
example of her father, Mifs Evans's
grief gradually fubfided into the tranquil
cheerfulnefs which naturally belonged to
her character. Her affection for her
mother fhowed itfelf in a tender attachment to her memory, and to every fubject connected with it; in a fteady imitation of her virtues, and a faithful obſervance

fervance of her precepts. The high heroic tone of her mind would have been wounded by a fuppofition, that love was more invulnerable than filial grief; and fhe certainly fo far fubdued her early preference, as to render it very little troublefome either to herfelf, or her friends. It did not incapacitate her for any duties, nor did it abforb any of her agreeable properties. She vifited Monteith in a few months after her mother's death, and delighted all who faw her with her good fenfe and agreeable vivacity. She even met Mr. Powerfcourt without betraying her fecret emotion to the moft fcrutinizing eye. She received him without either difcovering ftrong tranfport or adopting an artificial referve: and fhe bade him adieu with a voice fo little tremulous, that even lady Monteith could fcarcely detect her latent emotion.

It

It may be for the advantage of all love-fick young ladies, who fit under woodbine bowers or fhady beeches, or who walk by moonlight to hear nightingales and waterfalls, to learn by what means Mifs Evans was enabled to make fo refpectable a defence againft the purblind archer. In the firft place, fhe was conftantly employed; in the fecond, fhe never indulged in the dangerous pleafure of dwelling on the name and merits of her beloved, either in her converfation or in her letters, nor did fhe ever allow herfelf to complain of her hard lot. To prevent fuch repining, fhe often vifited the abodes of real mifery, and her attention was directed to that courfe of ftudy which is the reverfe of fentimental refinement.

Mr. Powerfcourt's fhort refidence at Monteith did not indicate a revival of that ftrong attachment to his lovely coufin

coufin which had given him fo much
unhappinefs. He had found abfence a
grand fpecific. Change of fcene, and
interefting objects of purfuit, had coun-
teracted the effect of love upon a mind,
which, though naturally calm and contemplative, was remarkably fufceptible
of deep impreffions, and addicted to a
penfive caft of thought. He had derived ftill further advantages from his
travels. His capacious underftanding
was eminently difpofed to receive all
the improvement which an extenfive
view of men and things could afford.
Habits of fociety wore off his natural
referve; and, as his youthful awkward-
nefs was owing to uncommon diffidence,
the fame circumftances which infpired a
modeft confcioufnefs in his own powers,
gave grace to his perfon and elegance
to his addrefs. Thus improved, Mifs
Evans might have found her deter-

9   mined

mined ftoicifm an ineffectual defence, if it had been long expofed to fo powerful an affailant. It may, on the other hand, be afked, if Mifs Evans's merit was not equally calculated to convince Henry, that female attractions may fafcinate in more than one form. I readily affent to the fuggeftion; but the prefence of lady Monteith did not admit the fair difplay of Lucy's powers; and that young lady contributed to her own defeat, by continually fufpecting that her friend led the difcourfe to fuch a topic purpofely to call her out, and that fuch or fuch an amufement was projected with a defign to leave her tête-à-tête with Mr. Powerfcourt. Her indignation at thefe ideas was fo warm, that inftead of being peculiarly brilliant, her determination to avoid being fingular could not prevent her from being uncommonly referved.

Henry,

Henry, on the other hand, confcious of the fragility of new-formed refolutions, was prevented from attending to the attractions of Mifs Evans by a fcrupulous watchfulnefs over his own heart, left it fhould deviate from thofe limits which he had prefcribed, in order to prevent lady Monteith from occupying more of his thoughts than common admiration juftified. He found, upon this vifit, that her wit and beauty were her leaft attractions. As a wife, as a mother, how admirable!—how enchanting as the prefiding directrefs of a large family!—how intelligent in her pleafures!—how prudent in her benevolence! Lord Monteith was uncommonly attentive to him, and fhowed a ftrong defire to contract a friendly intimacy. He talked of the pleafures of the chace, of the agreeable fociety of many gay carelefs fouls with whom he fpent feveral

happy

happy hours. Good heavens! could
the husband of Geraldine relish such low
amusements, and be worthy of her?
This thought kept Henry awake one
whole night, and the next morning he
determined to set off on a tour to the
Hebrides. Lord Monteith earnestly
pressed him to take his castle in his
return, and tempted him by offering to
introduce him to a party who proposed
spending a month in hunting the red
deer among the Grampian hills. Mr.
Powerscourt determined to avoid every
opportunity of drawing comparisons
dangerous to his integrity, and proposed
going to Ireland in his way back, with
an intention of paying a long-intended
visit to a particular friend.

The attachment of the Monteiths to
their northern residence seemed to in-
crease. My lord was sometimes re-
luctantly forced by the unavoidable
pressure

preſſure of parliamentary buſineſs to viſit London, and the counteſs generally embraced that opportunity of paying her duty at Powerſcourt. She once accompanied her lord to London, where lady Arabella, who was ſtill aſpiring to the character of a firſt-rate toaſt, was terrified at the appearance of rivalry with which the undiminiſhed charms of her lovely ſiſter threatened her, even in her own domain. Probably this viſit would have proved fatal to all the fond terms of affection which lady Arabella's letters had conſtantly expreſſed, had not family harmony been preſerved by the alarming illneſs of lady Monteith's eldeſt daughter who was left in Scotland, which ſummoned the affrighted mother from the haunts of pleaſure to the bed of pain. The child ſoon recovered under her watchful eye, and, though not inſenſible to the blandiſhments of adulation and

the feductions of pleafure, the grateful
heart of Geraldine forgot the lofs of
promifed amufement in the tranfport-
ing idea of the reftoration of her darling.

She was by this time the mother of
three daughters, all promifing and lovely.
The repeated difappointment of having
male iffue fomewhat difconcerted her
lord, yet the chagrin was not fo predominant as to caufe any diminution in
his attachment to his lady. Experience
taught him that her unvaried fweetnefs
was neceffary to his happinefs; and it
never occurred to him, that his peculiar
pleafures and purfuits were any impedi-
ments to hers. With too little reflection
ever to attend to his own defects, and
too little judgment to appreciate Geraldine's refined excellence, he gave an
unqualified affent to the affertions of his
acquaintance, and believed himfelf not
only

only a very happy, but alfo a very ex-, cellent hufband : and who among the lords of the creation will controvert that opinion, when they hear that his lady never contradicted him, and never found fault ?

I fhall leave to the fentimental part of my readers the tafk of commenting on the felfifhnefs and inelegance of lord Monteith's character; for, doubtlefs, they have long ago obferved, that his mind was caft in too grofs a mould to form the proper counterpart of Geraldine's; and I am ready to allow, that the diffimilarity muft be fatal to that pure felicity, the refult of a perfect congeniality in tafte and fentiment, which is always the reward of heroes and heroines, and is fometimes realized on the ftage of life. Such marked difproportion affords an unanfwerable argument to diffuade a young lady of ftrong feeling

E 2 from

from accepting an otherwife unexcep-
tionable offer; but fince no law, either
human or divine, permits it to diffolve
the marriage-bond, it cannot be urged
as an excufe for married wretchednefs,
unlefs fome moral defect or painful peculiarity in temper be fuperadded. Sen-
fibility may wifh that the ftock of mutual
happinefs may receive every agreeable
addition; but judgment will look abroad,
and, eftimating its own real fituation by
adverting to the lot of others, will find
reafons for content, particularly if humi-
lity whifper fomewhat of its own confcious deficiencies. I fpeak of general
wretchednefs, not of a momentary pang;
of a confirmed train of thinking, not of
a fudden reflection which reafon exa-
mines and rejects.

Long before the period of which I
am now treating, lady Monteith had
abandoned the impracticable fcheme of
arraying

arraying Acteon in the veftments of Apollo. The difcovery was painful to her vanity, which had taught her credulity to believe, that love and beauty are the true alchymifts that can tranfmute the bafeft metals into the pureft gold. But the fanguine hopes of youth do not fink under one difappointment. Her lord poffeffed many good qualities, and the uncontrolled power which he gave her over his fortune allowed her to execute every fcheme that her liberality fuggefted, and purfue her own tafte in its fulleft extent, provided fhe fpared him the irkfome tafk of being obliged to pay attention to her plans. As to any idea of being impeded in the execution of his own, the yielding gentlenefs of lady Monteith preferved her from making the mad attempt, which could only have been compared to " drinking up Eifel, or eating a crocodile."

E 3   If

If the fuggeftions of latent pride, or, to call it by its fofter name, confcious fuperiority, fometimes led her to think that fhe might have made a more congenial choice, returning tendernefs bade her ftart from the injurious fuggeftion, and fly to her colony or her plantations, which, prefenting the idea of her lord's indulgence, never failed to infpire complacency. The future was an ample field for hope, and fhe filled it with the moft agreeable images. She determined, by ftrictly attending to the education of her daughters, to bend their ductile minds to fuch purfuits as would enable her to find thofe colloquial pleafures in her maternal character, which had been withheld from her connubial portion.

Her thoughts were fometimes diverted from her favourite employment of framing fuch a plan of education as fhould

should infure fuccefs, to the contemplation of her Lucy's approaching happinefs, which every day rendered more
probable. Henry now generally refided
at Powerfcourt. His filial attentions
and agreeable manners enlivened fir
William's declining years; and his frequent opportunities of obferving Mifs
Evans convinced the countefs that her
beloved friend would gradually make
the conqueft fo important to her repofe,
in the manner which her ftrict fenfe of
delicacy and propriety required.

Bending under the enfeebling load of
time, but ftill tranquil, focial, and benevolent, the vifits of his beloved daughter feemed to renew fir William Powerfcourt's frail exiftence. Her countenance always befpoke happinefs, and he
forgave the negligent inadvertencies
vifible in lord Monteith's behaviour to
himfelf. "Old men and young lords,"

E 4   faid

said he, " can't be expected to suit one " another ; but he is kind to my child, " and that is sufficient."

I have now described those scenes of lady Monteith's life, in which, judging by the proper estimate of terrestrial good, she might be termed innocent and happy. An artful seducer combining with her master-passion reversed the pleasing prospects, and produced scenes which the following pages will develope. While I prosecute my arduous, and perhaps unpopular task, I rely on the lenity of those who sincerely regret the alarming relaxation of principle that too surely discriminates a declining age ; and I anticipate the candid allowances which they will make for any incidental defects in a well-meant endeavour to point out the tendency of several opinions now too generally diffused through every rank in society.

CHAP. XXII.

When Florio fpeaks, what virgin could withftand,
If gentle Damon did not fqueeze her hand?
With varying vanities, from every part,
They fhift the moving toyfhop of their heart;
Where wigs with wigs, with fwordknots fwordknots
    ftrive,
Beaus banifh beaus, and coaches coaches drive.

POPE.

WHILE lady Monteith exerted all the powers of her mind to enjoy fame and to diffufe happinefs, and her beloved Lucy Evans purfued the humbler but furer path of confcientioufly endeavouring to difcharge her duty to God and man, lady Arabella Macdonald, already embarked on the fea of gaiety and diffipation, applied all her thoughts to the attainment of two doubtful bleffings, a hufband and a coronet.

Difinterefted love is always a very favourite topic with youth and beauty.

E 5 After

After a fly obfervation, that pretty little
Geraldine might owe fome attractions
to Powerfcourt manor, fhe entreated
that her aunt would cautioufly fupprefs
the communication of her intended liberality; and, by hinting that jointures
always reverted to the family from which
they were granted, leave her to depend
upon her own radiant eyes for procuring
a fplendid eftablifhment. Oroondates
himfelf muft feel fome increafe of rapture, if, while his bride curtefied to him
after the performance of the marriage
ceremony, fhe at the fame time whifpered to him, that fhe was the acknowledged heirefs of four thoufand a year.
But if lady Arabella's hufband had any
fpark of Oroondates' gallantry, his rapture would folely refult from the delicate
referve of the lady, and he would undoubtedly reply, " Wealth cannot add
" to the tranfport I feel in calling you
" mine.

" mine. Employ the gaudy toys you
" mention in whatever way you pleafe;
" they will be no otherwife welcome to
" me, than as they promote your fatif-
" faction; for your heart is the only
" treafure which I wifh to retain."

In ages of very remote antiquity lovers
might talk in this ftyle; but as all au-
thentic memorials of thefe periods are
unhappily loft, fceptics are inclined to
doubt the actual exiftence of fuch very
difinterefted heroifm. Poor lady Arabella found that the fwains who flourifhed
in the clofe of the eighteenth century
were of a very different order of beings.
Perceiving that the firft London winter
produced more ftarers than adorers, fhe
fet out for Bath. Here Cupid in vain
continued to fhoot his arrows from her
eyes; the apathy of diffipation, more
invulnerable than the fhield of Minerva,
defended the intended victims. Idle-

nefs

nefs is faid to be the mother of Love;
but not the idlenefs of public places.
The lounging beaus, as they fauntered
arm in arm along the rooms, occafionally
cheered her fpirits with a paffing " How
" d'ye do," and then joined in protefting,
" that fhe was an immenfe fine girl, and
" that it was a fhame her father had not
" left her a fortune." The converfation
generally concluded with a laugh at the
repulfive ftate of lady Madelina, which
nobody feemed willing to infringe.

Lady Arabella now determined to try
the effect of rural fcenes; and, having
chofen the then fafhionable retirement
of Brighton as the probable refidence of
the vagrant loves, fhe perfuaded lady
Madelina, who went to Bath to fix a
flying gout, that her complaint was certainly fcorbutic, for which fea-bathing
was the only fpecific; and there at laft
the expected lover appeared in the form

of

of Sir Phelim O'Connaught, a very perfonable and very affiduous Irifh gentleman of good family, and unqueftionable honour. Though lady Arabella had protefted that fhe never would furrender to any thing beneath a coronet, Sir Phelim's addreffes were fo perfectly rhapfodical, that her heart feemed to flutter, when at this critical period its tranquillity was re-eftablifhed by the appearance of fome very ungenteel company,— I mean, a couple of fheriff's officers. Sir Phelim was fo fhocked at the audacity of fuch low villains intruding upon the haunts of gentlemen, that he was never feen abroad after their arrival. It afterwards appeared, that his attachment was not fo perfectly difinterefted as has been fuppofed; for that he had acquired fome knowledge of the difpofal of lady Madelina's jointure.

Lady

Lady Arabella joined in the laugh against her quondam adorer, and declared, that though certainly he was very specious, she had found him out in an instant, and was determined to divert herself with the fellow's ridiculous ways. She also added, that this was another proof how prudent it was in ladies of fortune to *conceal* their expectations, for *avowed* wealth was always exposed to degrading solicitations.

The winter campaign opened with eclat. A noble earl, whose affairs were a little deranged, laid siege in form, and the contest seemed to predict a happy issue, had not lady Madelina put the young general prematurely to the rout by inquiring after his rent-roll. Poor Arabella felt a little piqued; but no matter;—these were her happiest days;— she loved liberty, detested restraint, and
danced,

danced, laughed, and visited more than ever.

The defection of the noble earl was repaired by the attendance of two admirers, a viscount and a private gentleman, who started in the career of honourable love at the same instant. Hitherto her ladyship had been rather unfortunate in the character of her adorers; but her indecision in the present instance proved that she was actuated by motives widely different from the desire of connubial happiness. Lord Fitzosborne was an emaciated victim to licentious pursuits; Mr. Stanley was a youth of great promise, educated under the auspices of a worthy father. The aim of the former was to repair his shattered fortune, and to gratify his selfish vanity by exhibiting to the world a fine young woman in the character of his wife. The latter sought domestic tranquillity: the

beauty

beauty of lady Arabella had caught his
eye; her reported expectations far exceeded what his father would require in
pecuniary affairs; and, suppofing that a
young woman muft imbibe every virtue
under the aufpices of a perfon of lady
Madelina's ftrict decorum, he called her
levity innocent gaiety, her affectation
fprightlinefs of manner; and, fincerely
worfhipping the image he had fet up,
he ardently folicited his charmer's heart.
Though my difcoveries have enabled
my fagacious readers to conclude, that
the unfortunate Stanley was in purfuit
of a nonentity, an impaffioned lover could
not perceive that nothing but the ad-
verfe weight of a coronet prevented the
nodding fcale from preponderating in
his favour. True to the firft object of
her youthful defires, even the unworthi-
nefs of the giver could not in her idea
invalidate the gift. But the progrefs of
my

my hiftory now calls me from the portraiture of fafhionable love to the definition of polite friendfhip.

Though lady Arabella had very little of the fentimental in her character, fhe enjoyed the bleffing of a bofom friend. Her acquaintance with Mifs Campley commenced at her firft arrival in London. They dreffed in the fame uniform, went to the fame parties, laughed at the fame quizzes, and flirted with the fame beaus. But Mifs Campley, being the uncontrolled miftrefs of her own actions, foared to a character which fome reftrictions of lady Madelina's prevented her niece from adopting; I mean, that of a dafher. She drove four in hand, laid wagers, ran in debt, played at Pharo, and, though infinitely inferior to her friend in beauty, certainly laid claim to greater tafte and fpirit.

As

As the ladies had never interfered in each other's conquefts, their friendfhip was fixed as adamant. To own the truth, conqueft and Harriet Campley were no longer fynonimous terms. The gentlemen had long been more defirous of winning her money than her heart; and even few knight-errants would have poffeffed fufficient courage and difinterefted generofity, to refcue a diftreffed damfel from the harpy talons of the law at the rifk of their own certain ruin.

As the profpect of a fplendid eftablifhment became lefs probable, Mifs Campley's creditors were more clamorous; and, though fhe profeffed herfelf highly delighted with the expected eclat of an execution, her haggard countenance betrayed an agonized mind. The period of lady Arabella's double triumph proved the crifis of her fate; and the

unexpected

unexpected death of an only brother
changed her prospects from the gloom
of a prison to pleasure and affluence.

Lord Fitzosborne had known Miss
Campley from her earliest youth ; he
had often been at her parties, and had
won her money without wishing for a
further connexion ; but she now struck
him in a much more interesting point of
view. I do not mean to insinuate, that
he thought her mourning was particularly becoming, and suited to her complexion ; his lordship's taste led him to
pursue more solid advantages than a set
of features can promise. He was an
excellent calculator ; and, though he too
well understood the character of his present mistress, to fear the ultimate success
of his rival, he laid so much stress upon
the attractions of old dowagers, and the
frailty of vows of widowhood, that he
considered three thousand a-year in immediate

mediate poffeffion as better than four
thoufand in reverfion. But while he
continued rather unrefolved, the gout
fixed in lady Madelina's foot, and her
phyfician congratulated her upon an
event which would infallibly add at leaft
twenty years to her life. His lordfhip
waited for no other inducement to pay
his devoirs at the fhrine of the other
divinity. Mifs Campley's yielding gentlenefs forgave paft flights; and in lefs
than a month lady Arabella received
bride-cake and favours from the vifcountefs Fitzofborne.

This certainly was provoking; but
the faithful Stanley was a fure refource.
Here again lady Arabella's evil genius
met her to blaft her projects. Mr.
Stanley was not quite fo much in love
as to lofe all his powers of obfervation.
His charmer's conduct had been at leaft
doubtful. The encouraging fmiles which

had

had beamed full upon him ever fince
the vifcount's dereliction, were too fufpicious to be completely fafcinating;
and he thought a journey into the country would at leaft fhow his miftrefs, that
he was not one of Cupid's tame votaries.
In his take-leave vifit he made fome
further difcoveries into her ladyfhip's
character; and while he made his final
bow, his regret at his difappointment
was foftened by the confcioufnefs of
efcaping that worft of evils, a diffipated
unprincipled wife.

Lady Arabella had charming fpirits.
She laughed at the vanity of the men,
creatures who fuppofed themfelves of
confequence; and, intimating that
though fhe had private reafons for re-
jecting Lord Fitzofborne, they were not
of a nature to influence her deareft
Harriet's choice, fhe waited with impatience for the return of the bride and
bridegroom

bridegroom to town. She flew to make the wedding vifit, gave in her card, was admitted, and congratulated the happy pair in terms equally fincere with the profeffions of efteem and friendfhip which fhe received in return. The vifcountefs now infifted that fhe fhould be her conftant vifitor, and ftrongly urged her not to mope herfelf at home during her aunt's confinement. Lady Arabella declared, that her ladyfhip was the only good Chriftian that fhe had talked to for a long time; and that it really would be charity to take her out of the fphere of flannels and fomentations. They agreed to go to every place where there was any thing to be feen. Lady Fitzofborne delared with a fmile, that even if her lord was fometimes of the party fhe had a foul too capacious for jealoufy; and her equally liberal friend, with a loud laugh, obferved, that fhe was not

yet

yet arrived at the age of envy and her laſt prayers. Lady Fitzoſborne's ſpeech needs no explanation; but the wit of lady Arabella's retort conſiſted in an alluſion to the circumſtance of her dear friend's being ten years older than herſelf.

The friends were conſtantly together, except when the myſteries of Pharo im‑poſed a temporary ſeparation. I have already ſaid, that lady Madelina's ſevere notions reſtricted ſome of her niece's propenſities; but this was not the only thing that prevented Arabella from being caught in that ruinous vortex from whoſe fatal contact peace and honour muſt never hope to eſcape. Lord Fitzoſborne was, ſince his mar‑riage, become a man of character, a lover of decorum, and a conſiderate obſerver of pecuniary advantages. For‑tune ſeldom beſtows her gifts ſingly, and

and fince her acceffion to her brother's
eftate, his lady had an amazing run of
luck. She was not only able to difcharge her own debts of honour, but to
pay fome of his; and this was the only
circumftance which could at all reconcile his notions of propriety with her
infraction of the laws of her country.
His thoughts were now turned to the
advantageous eftablifhment of his brother Edward Fitzofborne, who had refided many years abroad upon the limited portion of a younger fon. His lordfhip had been affured by many refpectable travellers, that this young gentleman was an honour to his name, poffeffed of elegant manners, uncommon
erudition, and an irreproachable character: that he appeared in the firft
circles, correfponded with the firft literary characters of the age, and was fit-
ted to move in the moft exalted fphere.

The

The noble viſcount's fraternal tenderneſs yearned at the recital. He determined to ſend for him to England, to
get him into parliament, to puſh him in
the world, and to marry him to a fortune. It was with a reference to this
deſign that he prohibited the viſcounteſs
from initiating her friend in her private
myſteries.

Mr. Fitzoſborne received his brother's ſummons to England with regret, and begged that he might be permitted to remain at Paris, where he
was juſt then contemplating the ſublime
ſpectacle of a great nation emancipating
itſelf from the fetters of tyranny and
ſuperſtition. It was, he ſaid, his wiſh
to continue abroad, to watch the pro-
greſs of events that would enlarge his
mind, and render him ſtill worthier of
the office of a Britiſh legiſlator. The
peer, whoſe ideas were equally liberal,

granted

granted the requeſt; and, depending
upon his own watchfulneſs, and the
chicanery of his lady, to prevent the
glittering gold-fiſh that he wiſhed to
entrap from eſcaping their net, he permitted Mr. Fitzoſborne to proſecute
his ſtudies, till the coercive meaſures
which democracy was compelled to
adopt obliged even the lovers of freedom to take ſhelter in the legal deſ-
potiſm of Old England.

CHAP. XXIII.

—'Tis not impossible
But one, the wicked'st caitiff on the ground,
May seem as shy, as grave, as just, as absolute,
As Angelo; even so may Angelo
In all his dressings, characts, titles, forms,
Be an arch villain.

SHAKESPEARE.

LADY ARABELLA was with her dear Harriet when Mr. Fitzosborne unexpectedly arrived. He had narrowly escaped the guillotine, had passed the sea in a fishing-boat, and had encountered so many perils, that his admiration of that meretricious liberty whose distinguishing code is equality of wretchedness, was rather abated. "Hair-breadth 'scapes" are very interesting to most ladies, and Mr. Fitzosborne's powers of recitation were unrivalled. His per-

F 2

son

son had every charm, his manner every advantage. Lady Arabella looked, listened, admired, and went home vastly rejoiced, that such a delightful young man had escaped the odious democrats.

The next morning, at an early hour, lady Fitzosborne rushed into her friend's dressing-room. " Enchanting news!
" my dearest Bella," said she; " we
" shall never more be distressed for
" want of a cecisbeo. My lord has
" asked Edward to live with us till he
" forms an establishment of his own.
" Is not he a divine fellow? And this
" morning he looks more resistless than
" ever. Such spirit! such information!
" It would have been a shame to have
" had him confounded with a parcel of
" emigrant desperadoes. He spoke
" very fine things of you, my dear; he
" seems quite struck, I assure you. If
" you were but a little more Greek in
" your drapery, he declared, you would
                                " have

" have put him in mind of La Liberté
" on the day of deification, who was
" the handfomeft courtefan in all
" Paris.

"But, blefs me!" continued the
Britifh peerefs, looking at her watch,
" how I trifle. I vow I have fifty
" vifits to make this morning. Good
" bye! I fhall call upon you for the
" opera this evening. I long to fhow
" Edward the new houfe. O, I declare
" I have not had the humanity to in-
" quire after *aunty*; but I can't ftay to
" hear now. You'll tell me to-night all
" the procefs of the foot, and the doctor.
" Sparkle, my love: Edward is amaz-
" ingly fond of wit."

Pity is faid to be near akin to Love:
and when blended with admiration, and
infpired by the idea of awakening reci-
procal fentiments in the bofom of another, it may certainly be ftyled the

F 3   parent

parent of the foft infatuation. Though
philofophy was Mr. Fitzofborne's chief
forte, he did not belong to the fchool
of Diogenes. One prime article in his
creed was, that an adept did not
ftudy to lefs advantage for poffeffing
the good things of this life. Indeed,
as his views were not very clear on the
fubject of a future ftate, he confidered
it to be his bounden duty to embrace
all the advantages which the prefent
afforded. Gentlemen of his principles
do not mean by their general declama-
tions in favour of liberality, honour,
and philofophical equanimity, to convey the precife idea, that fuch qualities
are indifpenfably requifite in their own
characters : for they know, that the exterior refemblance exactly anfwers the
fame end. Superficial obfervers (and
the major part of mankind belong to
this clafs) will give you credit for poffeffing

feffing a virtue, provided you are
loud in your cenfures of an oppofite
vice.   Good notions of public liberty
give the licence which permits you to
be a private tyrant.   The daring atheift
and fophifticating fceptic may alike
fhelter under the veil of religious moderation : and provided the words honour,
fentiment, and philanthropy, be upon
your tongue, you may difturb the repofe
of mankind, either individually or col-
lectively, with impunity.

   To illuftrate the analogy in the prefent inftance : Could the enlarged foul
of Edward Fitzofborne have heard the
fhameful tale of mercenary indigence
concealing difguft under the mafk of
admiration to entrap the wealth of ina-
nity into a degrading connexion, without expreffing the moft generous emotion ?   How would his ftrong feelings
have revolted at the fight of thofe fordid

fhackles

ſhackles which militated againſt the natural liberty of man, and the idea of
that *confirmed habit* of diſſimulation
which annihilated his ſuppoſed inherent
perfection. He could certainly have
been very eloquent upon theſe themes,
if they referred to the conduct of a me-
thodiſt or a formaliſt; but when applied
to his own concerns it was ſoon ad-
juſted. The girl wanted a huſband, the
gentleman a fortune; the balance,
therefore, was as nicely trimmed as the
moſt equalizing ſpirit could deſire.
This conſideration might have been
further uſeful, as it neceſſarily diſſolved
all ties of gratitude; but Mr. Fitzoſborne had long before diſcovered,
that private gratitude is inconſiſtent
with public virtue.

Lady Arabella had no doubt that her
wit and beauty held out ſufficient attractions to a gentleman ſo profeſſedly
diſ-

disinterested as her new admirer (for he assumed that character in a few days); and she did not even attempt to misconstrue his behaviour, or to disguise the pleasure which she received from his addresses. Fitzosborne was not a sensualist. Beauty was to him a mere abstract quality, particularly when associated to the idea of a wife. He had been too long accustomed to the coruscations of real genius, to bestow more than a languid smile on lady Arabella's jejune *bons mots*. Even that languid smile was soon converted into saturnine silence. Her character was too superficial to interest his attention. He discovered her foibles, detected her artifices, and despised her understanding, in the first month of his courtship. She was too easy a conquest for his ambition; and nothing but the reluctance which he felt at the thought of being de-

F 5   pendent.

pendent upon his brother could have reconciled him to the idea of an alliance.

Perceiving her heart irredeemably enthralled, (though in this opinion he was fomewhat duped by his own vanity,) he began to act the preconcerted part. He was now no longer the affiduous lover, but the man of firm honour and inviolable integrity, incapable of betraying unfufpicious innocence, or of feducing a young lady from the duty which fhe owed to the protecting kindnefs of a venerable relation. Lady Arabella unwarily acknowledged, that her aunt was inclined to fufpect a mercenary motive for his addreffes, and this drew from him an exordium on the purity and difinterestedness of his attachment, with a declaration, that though it would glow in his breast with unabated fervour, yet he had rather perifh the untimely victim

of

of defpair, than juftify lady Madelina's
fentiments by a departure from that
ftrict honour which had ever been the
ruling principle of his life. " No!
" lady Arabella," continued he, while
the aftonifhed lady was incapable of in-
terrupting him, " the enlightened mind
" needs no other incentive than confcious
" rectitude to enable it always to act as
" it ought. I can fupport penury, exile,
" or even the lofs of you; but I cannot
" fupport difgrace. Lady Madelina has
" injured me by her unjuft fufpicions.
" She has cruelly ftriven to infufe her
" own narrow prejudices into a mind
" which I hoped was incapable of an
" illiberal doubt. How can I be fure
" that fhe has not fucceeded? Your
" eyes, your manner, evince lefs confi-
" dence than they were wont; and my
" alarmed heart anticipates the gloomy
" period, when referve and fufpicion

F 6   " fhall

" shall chill the sentiments of pure, in-
" genuous, disinterested love. Sooner
" than such mischiefs shall fall upon me,
" I will resign you, madam, and even
" at this moment tear myself from you
" for ever."

" I cannot see for what reason," returned the lady, whom this vehement
oratory had driven from her usual re-
source of playing with her fan or ad-
justing her dress; " I declare, Mr. Fitz-
" osborne, I can't bear to hear you talk
" so." If the declamation of the gentleman was pathetic, the silence of the lady
was no less so; for it proceeded from a
flood of tears.

After a few forced compliments to
this trait of feeling, Edward resumed
the discourse on the subject of the claims
of duty, which were, he said, often incompatible with those of the heart. In
the conclusion he seemed a little softened

on

on the harsh subject of eternal separation : but then lady Madelina must come forward, unsay her former cruel aspersions, and with her own hand lead her niece to the altar.

Reveal then, ye immortal Muses! who inspire great designs, what means achieved the glorious task of subjugating lady Madelina's narrow suspicions, and restoring to her mind the beautiful simplicity of nature. Neither the resplendent character nor the exalted birth of a Fitzosborne could have gained the arduous victory, if powers supernal had not intervened. First, Venus, queen of gentle devices! taught her prototype, lady Arabella, the use of feigned sighs, artificial tears, and studied faintings : while Esculapius descended from Olympus, and, assuming the form of a smart physician, stepped out of an elegant chariot, and on viewing the patient,

after

after three fagacious nods, whifpered to the trembling aunt, that the young lady's diforder, being purely mental, was beyond the power of the healing art. Reduced to the dire alternative of refigning the fair fufferer to a hufband or to the grave, the relenting lady Madelina did not long hefitate. The refentment of injured honour was appeafed by expreffions which more nearly refembled conceffions than any that her ladyfhip had ever uttered; and Arabella foon appeared again in public with very little diminution of her charms, notwithftanding her late alarming illnefs.

It muft now be obferved, that Mr. Fitzofborne was entirely paffive through the whole of this affair. Young ladies are apt to miftake general politenefs for fignificant attentions, and gentlemen are not blamable for the tinder-like fufceptibility of their hearts. As foon as

lady

lady Arabella's preference was vifible, he became more referved in his conduct, as all his friends could witnefs. Nay, he had even gone fo far as to recall to her mind thofe principles of action, which he gloried in avowing to be the acknowledged energies of his foul. Her unhappy predilection filenced his obfervations. What then! could he be blamed, or ought he to have fuppreffed that flow of liberal benevolence which a full heart prompted him to pour forth, and which undoubtedly captivated the amiable fair one? Recollecting the motives which an illiberal world might affign to his behaviour, he believed he ought to have done fo, but it was now too late. The public knew the reft. He trufted that the lady had fufficiently confulted her own happinefs to ftudy the peculiarities of his character. It was above difguife and abhorrent of reftriction.

ftriction. If fhe had been miftaken, he deplored the confequences. But as the ftrong characteriftics of nature were engraven on his mind with indelible force, he could not be expected to change.

The claffical embellifhments of the heroic ages gave infinite advantages to defcriptive narrations, to which the cold copyift of modern manners can never afpire. How animating is the perfonification of winged loves, and choral graces, white-armed nymphs ftrewing flowers, and fportive fawns chanting an epithalamium, Juno on her radiant car, and Hymen in his faffron mantle! What can the brighteft imagination do with fuch uncouth figures as lawyers in tie-wigs, with their green bags and parchments, or even a little painted French milliner with her band-box? The Britifh like the Grecian bride

bride offers facrifices, but not to the deities of Complacence and nuptial Harmony—Her devoirs are too frequently directed to the fhrines of Fafhion and Vanity; and the merits of the villa, the town-houfe, the jewels and the nuptial paraphernalia are difcuffed with all imaginable fcrupulofity, while the lover's character is overlooked. He on the other hand is too bufy in balancing the chances of the lady's fortune againft her father's demand of fettlement, and the poffibility of *privately* clearing off his moft preffing incumbrances, to confider his deftined wife in any other light than as a neceffary appendage, which entitles him to take poffeffion.

Every fcheme preparatory to lady Arabella's intended nuptials was conducted with the greateft decorum. Lady Madelina herfelf undertook the bufinefs of

of directing the fettlements; and Mr.
Fitzofborne, contenting himfelf with
the power of putting a negative upon her
determinations fhould the terms be unreafonable, fhowed little of the alacrity
and rapture which a deftined bridegroom
is expected to affume. Various delays
arofe to retard the concluding ceremony;
and the good-natured world began to
doubt, whether the gentleman was moft
unwilling to part with his liberty, or
lady Madelina with her fortune.

Lady Arabella enjoyed, in its fulleft
extent, the confequence which her prefent fituation gave her. Some mornings
fhe went a fhopping to cheap ware-
houfes; at others fhe was waited upon
by different tradefmen at home: fhe
ordered and counter-ordered; bought
and returned; thought this monftrous
pretty, and that monftrous frightful;
gave as much trouble as her rank would
                                        poffibly

poffibly enable her to impofe, and then complained of the impertinence and impofition of trades-people.

During one of the delays, which, as I have already obferved, retarded the lighting of the Hymeneal torch, lady Arabella recollected, that her conqueft over fcience, philofophy, and genius, was infinitely more arduous than Geraldine's eafy fafcination of fuch a thoughtlefs random youth as her brother. It next occurred to her, that fhe fhould prodigioufly like to mortify her fifter's pretended fuperiority in fenfe and talents, by exhibiting a Fitzofborne in her chains. The thought of an excurfion to Scotland as foon as fhe was married, muft be attended with many inconveniencies; and, what was ftill more repugnant to her feelings, with the renunciation of much eclat and fplendor. Befide, it was moft defirable that the

exhi-

exhibition fhould be made while fhe was invefted with full plenitude of power. An exprefs was, therefore, difpatched to Scotland to requeft, that a brother's hand would confign her's to a hufband every way worthy of his alliance. The letter concluded with an acknowledgment of tender trepidations, which nothing but the prefence of her Geraldine could allay. Lady Madelina's increafing infirmities rendered her unfit to be the depofitory of her forrows; and her dear lady Fitzofborne, her only friend, was infinitely too much in the interefts of her happy brother, as fhe ftyled him, to treat her apprehenfive heart with fufficient delicacy.

The Monteiths readily complied with a fummons which indicated a perfect renewal of domeftic harmony. Though the yellow teint of early autumn had juft diffufed a more picturefque

turefque appearance over the romantic banks of Loch Lomond, and announced the joyous feafon of the "hound and horn," a dangerous fall-from his horfe had given the earl a tranfient difguft to field fports; and though the blooming countefs was by no means weary of her rural enjoyments and occupations, fhe was too young, and too lovely, to reject an invitation to partake of the elegant varieties which London afforded. She intended to act in this, as fhe had done at her preceding vifits; to tafte the Circean cup with moderation, and then to retire with dignity from the fafcinating banquet. But there are periods, when, if left to its own ftability, the firmeft foot would fail; and the beft regulated mind, deprived of fuperior guidance, may often deplore its own depravity.

CHAP. XXIV.

—— He reads much,
He is a great obferver, and he looks
Quite through the deeds of men.

SHAKESPEARE.

LADY ARABELLA prepared her lover
for the arrival of the expected ftrangers.
" I would not fay fo to other people,"
faid fhe, " becaufe one ought to fhow
" refpect to one's relations. But to be
" fure the Monteiths are the very odd-
" eft creatures in the world. My bro-
" ther is well enough for one of your
" fox-hunters, as they call them; but
" the lady, O! fhe is fo fine and fo fen-
" fible, and fo cautious, and fo——I
" don't know how——vaftly difagreeable;
" I affure you, you will be highly di-
" verted with her: pray obferve her,
" and tell me all you think of her; for
" I fhall not take any thing ill that you
                                    " fay.

" fay. She is prodigioufly wife, you
" muft know. I hate wife people, at
" leaft fuch wife people as fhe is. Play
" her off; I fhall be vaftly entertained."

Developing characters was Mr. Fitzofborne's favourite amufement; and it
was one of his topics of complaint, that
he had never fince his return to England
met with any perfon that was worth ftu-
dying. But after he had feen the Monteiths, he did not repeat that opinion.
The interefting beauty of the countefs,
her apparent happinefs, and vifible influence over her lord's affections, which
even his carelefs manners could not difguife, excited in the philofophic mind
of Fitzofborne nearly the fame emotions
as thofe which the arch Apoftate felt on
viewing Adam and Eve in Paradife:
and, like him,

———— " Afide he turn'd
" For envy; yet with jealous leer malign
" Ey'd them afkance."

In

In one particular the refemblance was
certainly incomplete.   The fuperior intelligence of the fallen angel knew, that
the happinefs which he intended to
deftroy was real.   Habitually fceptical,
Fitzofborne doubted.   He watched the
varying turns of Geraldine's animated
countenance, analyzed her manner and
her expreffions with the hope of difcovering fomething to convince him that
fhe was only a polifhed diffembler.   For
it was utterly repugnant to all his received ideas, that affection could really
fubfift between perfons of difcordant
habits, or that principle could fupply the
place of attachment, and give equal
uniformity to the conduct.

The joyous occafion which had fummoned him to town gave lord Monteith
a prodigious flow of fpirits; and he
certainly always appeared to leaft advantage when moft inclined to take the

lead

lead in converfation. When he was
difpofed to talk, he never confidered
how far the indulgence of his own humour was agreeable to the company.
His difcourfe could only be interefting
to himfelf and lady Madelina; for it
related to his own caftle; how much he
and Geraldine had improved it; how
popular they were among their neighbours; and how they fpent their time.
He faid many ridiculous things, and
uttered many expreffions indicative of
good nature and benevolence; yet,
though he certainly did not intend it,
retirement had transformed the gallant
Monteith; and his wife and his little girls
were ftill the heroines of his tale. Meantime the countefs appeared to be engaged
by lady Arabella's frivolity. Her eye
indeed frequently reverted to her lord.
But whether her attention proceeded

from

from anxiety or affection even Fitzofborne could not difcover.

His lordfhip at length grew tired;
his fifter had exhaufted her hyperbolical
rapture at this happy interview; and the
converfation changing to places of public amufement allowed fome opening to
the countefs. The opera was mentioned.
Lady Arabella declared, that the new
grand ballet was fo charming, that it
abfolutely threw her into hyfterics. " I
" proteft," continued fhe, " I don't
" think I fhall dare to go again, for
" it makes me downright nervous the
" next day."

" I congratulate you," faid lady Monteith, " on the acquifition of a new
" pleafure. You had ufed to profefs
" yourfelf an enemy to mufic."

" O! I hate it ftill in a room, or
" where there is but one performer.
                                    " But

" But the opera is fo different. There
" the lights, and the company, and the
" fcenes, and the dreffes, do fo increafe
" the effect! And the dances are fo fine,
" and every body is fo overcome, and
" one feels fo fafcinated !"

" The mufic I have been lately ac-
" cuftomed to," refumed Geraldine,
" is in a very different ftyle. An old
" Highlander playing upon his bagpipe,
" and the voices of two or three Scotch
" girls chaunting one of their fimple
" ditties, which reverberates among our
" rocks, convey to me a more perfect
" idea of the powers of melody, than the
" fcenes you defcribe. And though I
" hope frequently to vifit the opera
" while in London, I much doubt whe-
" ther my fenfibility can be fo ftrongly
" affected there as it has frequently been
" during my evening rambles about
" James-town."

G 2 " I hope,

" I hope, madam," said lady Madelina, " that your ladyſhip never *walks* " beyond the limits of your own park."

" James-town is but a little way from " the caſtle," replied the counteſs, not immediately entering into the force of this obſervation ; " I go there moſt days, " and the walk is much pleaſanter than " the drive."

" It is very right, niece," obſerved lady Madelina, in a tone of ſtricter authority, " that you ſhould aſſiſt your " dependants ; but you ſhould do it like " a gentlewoman ; and too frequent in- " tercourſe breeds familiarity and con- " tempt."

" I have fortunately not found fami- " liarity and contempt ſynonimous," reſumed lady Monteith, who, though generally ſilently acquieſcent, ſeemed on the preſent occaſion diſpoſed to defend her own conduct. " I appear to my " colony

" colony in one uniform character; and
" however frequent my visits, or in
" whatever style I make them, a friend
" is not unwelcome, and a benefactress
" need not fear contempt. Continual
" intercourse creates a mutual interest.
" I thoroughly enter into their characters.
" Beside, I acquire much knowledge in
" various particulars, which those who
" are not personally acquainted with
" humble life can never accurately pos-
" sess."

" And of what use is that knowledge?"
inquired lady Madelina.

" It may be applied to various pur-
" poses. It teaches me the value of
" time. Because while we are studying
" amusements to get rid of what we feel
" to be an incumbrance, the poverty of
" the labourer makes him conscious of
" its importance. He knows that he
" cannot waste an hour without finding

G 3   " his

" his daily food abridged. And when
" I fee the œconomical contrivances
" which neceffity teaches, the humble
" comforts which ftand inftead of lux-
" uries, and the cheerful patience with
" which real inconveniencies are borne
" by thofe who know no happier lot, I
" cannot (at leaft immediately) become
" faftidious and extravagant."

" The unfortunate fenfibility of my
" temper," faid lady Arabella, " would
" never permit me to frequent fuch
" places. You certainly muft have very
" ftrong nerves, fifter. I proteft, when
" I have feen feveral little dirty, ftarved,
" naked children, peeping out of thofe
" fmoky hovels which ftand by the road
" fide, I have often thought that it
" would be great mercy to fhoot them,
" as one does worn-out horfes."

" To fhoot them !" exclaimed moft
of the company.

" Yes !"

" Yes!" refumed lady Arabella; " for
" only think what a miferable life theirs
" muft be."

" Did you never fee any of thefe poor
" little creatures merry?" inquired the
countefs.

" O yes! the little favages grinned
" fometimes, and jumped about like
" monkies; and with juft as much
" fenfe; for if they thought at all, they
" muft be miferable."

Geraldine recollected the fentiment,
that " where ignorance is blifs," it is
both cruel and foolifh to impart a knowledge which difcovers wretchednefs. But
while fhe was confidering how beft to
point out thofe comforts which opulence
and intelligence might impart to the
poor, without creating defires unfuitable
to their ftations, her reflections were
interrupted by an harangue from Fitzofborne.

G 4   " Nature,

" Nature, madam," said he, addreſſing himſelf to lady Arabella, " is not " a niggard; though the imbecility of " political inſtitutions and the corrupt " ſtate of ſociety frequently confine her " beneficent views. Theſe infant ſavages " enjoy bleſſings to which perhaps their " oppreſſors are ſtrangers. Health, " natural liberty, exemption from care, " and a happy ignorance of all the reſtraints which cuſtom impoſes, and all " the falſe indulgencies which affluence " requires. Their manners are unde- " praved, their inclinations unſophiſti- " cated. I ſhould think theſe obſcure " cots the choſen abodes of innocence " and virtue."

" That is rather too liberal a con- " jecture," returned lady Monteith, beaming upon the ſuppoſed champion of the equal dealings of Providence a complacent ſmile. " My long reſidence
" in

" in retirement allows me pofitively to
" contradict the popular notion, that
" the country is the feat of Arcadian
" happinefs and purity, though much
" may be done to ameliorate the con-
" dition of the lower claffes of fociety;
" and I am convinced, that refiding
" among them is one of the moft pro-
" bable means of effecting that import-
" ant defign."

" I perfectly agree with your lady-
" fhip's fentiments, particularly when
" the poor, like the fortunate vaffals of
" Monteith, may contemplate exalted
" rank without fear of imbibing exotic
" vices." The countefs blufhed, and
bowed at this compliment, without recollecting, that it might be intended for
her lord. Fitzofborne watched the fudden emotion. " Can vanity," faid he
to himfelf, " be the ruling foible? If

" it

" it be, the fmothered flame fhall
" blaze."

Lord Monteith now took part in the
converfation. " I hope, Sir, you mean
" to put your own principles in practice,
" and that we fhall be very good friends
" when you come to refide at Kinloch
" Caftle. It is within eighty miles of
" us, and we may frequently join in
" parties upon the lakes and the moors.
" I was there once. I thought it a hor-
" rid place with its canopied ftate beds,
" and worm-eaten tapeftry ; but you
" will give it a more agreeable air when
" you live there."

" Live there !" fhrieked lady Arabella. " What ! live at Kinloch Caftle ?
" What a barbarous idea !"

" O you are thinking of times of old,
" poor Bella. Yes ! they were barba-
" rous, I'll grant. But it will be very
                              " different

" different when you shall be living
" there with a good husband, from what
" it was when you wanted to set off from
" it in search of one. Poor Bella! I
" remember your peeping through the
" painted glass between the huge stone
" window-frames, and wondering, whe-
" ther the object that looked black
" at a great distance was a cow or a
" gentleman. Poor Bella! If you are
" any thing of a knight-errant, Fitzof-
" borne; you would have liked to have
" seen her shut up in that castle, like an
" enchanted lady, waiting for some gal-
" lant Longsword to set her at liberty.
" But I suppose Longsword was be-
" nighted, or set upon by Saracens, for
" he never found his way to the castle——
" Did he, Bella?"

My lord had now recovered the conversation; and no common effort could
get it out of his hands, till lady Arabella

very

very gravely told him, that his raillery
was misplaced. His lordship then, start-
ing up, gave his sister a good-humoured
kiss, declared that he did not mean to
displease her, promised to say no more
about the castle that nobody could get
out of, or the knight that never could get
in; and whispering her, that he then
thought her the prettiest prisoner he ever
saw in his life, he summoned the countess
and hurried her back to Portland-place.

Lady Arabella scarcely waited till
they were out of sight, to ask if they
were not strange creatures.

"The countess," said Fitzosborne,
"is most amazingly beautiful."

"She must be very much improved
"then," returned lady Arabella; "for
"it used to be doubted where she was
"even pretty. But I believe gentlemen
"who have lived much abroad have a
"*singular* taste in beauty."

"There

"There are some forms," said Fitzosborne, bowing with a significant air,
" which would be esteemed lovely in
" every region. Lady Monteith's chief
" beauty is the sparkling intelligence of
" her countenance ; for certainly her
" features are not regular."

" No," rejoined her ladyship a little
appeased, " her features are not regular ;
" and some people will call that intelli-
" gence in her countenance conceit."

" Is she counted vain ?"

" Insufferably so. It is her ruling
" foible. Every body who is acquainted
" with her knows it. I wonder you did
" not discover it."

Fitzosborne promised to consider her
character with deeper attention at the
next opportunity. " If vanity," said he
to himself, " be indeed her predominant
" fault, it is impossible that her apparent
" happiness can be sincere. The vanity
" of

" of a fuperior mind is not gratified by
" common incenfe; and Monteith feems
" too thoughtlefs to difcern her peculiar
" excellencies, and too felf-engroffed to
" give them their appropriate praife.   I'
" fufpect that his perfonal advantages
" attracted her inexperience, and that
" her judgment now fecretly reprobates
" the premature choice."

Lord Monteith's opinion of the intended difpofal of his fifter was, that it
was a very well-fchemed thing.   " She
" was juft a fit match," faid he, " for a
" younger brother.   Fitzofborne feems
" to have a great deal of fenfe, and we
" all know that Arabella is not one of
" king Solomon's family.   She will,
" perhaps, prove a little refractory at
" firft; but he will conduct himfelf
" cleverly, and foon convince her that
" the hufband is the fuperior character.
" You think fo, Geraldine, don't you?"
                                " O, un-

" " O, undoubtedly !" But, with what-ever certainty the countefs could fpeak of her own fituation, fhe felt extremely doubtful as to the happy iffue of lady Arabella's profpects. In fpite of the referve of her lover's character, their diffimilarity was evident. She was tri-fling, fuperficial, felfifh, and unguarded : with refpect to Fitzofborne, whenever the thick veil with which he chofe to obfcure himfelf admitted a cafual dif-covery, fuperior intelligence and libe-rality of fentiment were apparent. " I " know," faid Geraldine to herfelf, " that Arabella's temper is impetuous, " her prejudices are rooted, and her " views of connubial happinefs are too " fuperficial to make her even wifh to " affimilate her tafte to that of her huf- " band's, or to affign any merit to com- " placent acquiefcence. His enlarged " underftanding muft difcover her fool-

" ifh

"ifh pertinacity; and the generous feel-
"ing that always accompanies a liberal
"mind will be perpetually wounded by
"the contracted ideas of a felfifh heart.
"Her ridiculous opinion of the conftant
"incenfe which beauty demands pre-
"cludes all hope of her improvement.
"She will be continually requiring a
"flatterer, and he a companion. I am
"certain, that even now he ftrongly
"feels the difproportion of their minds.
"What harfh expreffions did he utter
"againft the oppreffors of the poor.
"They were, doubtlefs, pointed at her
"extravagant notions, which feemed to
"degrade them from the rank of ra-
"tional creatures. Indeed, though his
"mercenary defign fomewhat debafes
"his character, I pity Mr. Fitzofborne.
"He appears to be well worthy of a
"happier fate."

The

The chain of her reflections was here broken by his lordſhip's obſerving, that ſhe was as dull and as bad company as his future brother-in-law.

CHAP. XXV.

Calm thinking villains, whom no faith can fix,
Of crooked councils and dark politics.

POPE.

FITZOSBORNE called to return the honour of lord Monteith's visit just at the time when his lordship was gone out on some important business. This engagement had been discussed the preceding evening, but philosophers are very apt to be absent. He inquired if the countess was at home, and on sending in his name he was admitted. There could be no impropriety in receiving a visit from a gentleman who was soon to become a relation; and Geraldine had been sufficiently interested by his appearance to be anxious to know if the estimate that she had formed of his character was just.

Previous

Previous to his arrival, she had been amusing herself with a harp which had lain silent for some years. It had been new strung by an eminent hand, and was become capable of producing the most ravishing harmony. Fitzosborne was an idolator of music. The skill of the countess was too well known to admit of disqualifying speeches. She readily complied with his request to exhibit the powers of her instrument, and after a graceful prelude accompanied it with her voice in the following sonnet:

SONNET TO MAY.

Come May, the empire of the earth assume,
  Be crown'd with flowers as universal queen;
  Take from fresh budded groves their tender
    green,
Bespangled with Pomona's richest bloom,
And form thy vesture. Let the sun illume
  The dew-drops glittering in the blue serene,
  And let them hang, like orient pearls, between
Thy locks besprent with Flora's best perfume.

Attend

Attend your fovereign's fteps, ye balmy gales !
  O'er her ambrofial floods of fragrance pour ;
Let livelier verdure animate the vales,
  And brighter hues embellifh every flower ;
And hark, the concert of the woodland hails,
  All gracious May! thy prefence, and thy power.

She enforced the laft line with the whole
compafs of her melodious voice. The
apartment reverberated with the magic
founds. She paufed. Fitzofborne feemed loft in fpeechlefs ecftafy. He raifed
his eyes, fuffufed with tears, and they
met thofe of the countefs.—He retired
to the window to recover from his emotion, while fhe formed the ineffectual
wifh, that Arabella had poffeffed a mind
capable of eftimating and rewarding fuch
refined fenfibility.

It was fome moments before Fitzofborne was able to renew the converfation. At length he hefitatingly arti-
culated, " You devote many hours
" every day to this charming fcience ?"

" No,

" No, indeed! I very feldom play,
" unlefs to perfect myfelf in a new tune,
" or to amufe lord Monteith."

" Is lord Monteith fond of mufic ?"

" Paffionately fo."

" I did not fufpect it.   Of what
kind ?"

" Every kind : from the loftieft
" compofitions of Handel to the fim-
" pleft ftrains of ruftic harmony.   But
" I prefume, fir, your tafte is more dif-
" criminating ; and being formed upon
" the refined Italian model, it requires
" artful combination and ftriking con-
" traft."

" It requires, madam, fuch an exalted
" gratification as it has juft enjoyed."
He then rofe, as if intending to take
leave, when a miniature of Lucy Evans,
which hung over the chimney glafs, appeared firft to attract his eye ; and he
                              exclaimed,

exclaimed, " You paint, I know ; do
" you take likeneffes ?"

" Very bad ones," faid the countefs,
handing to him the picture. " And
" when you view that juvenile perform-
" ance with attention, you will fay fo.
" But it is highly valuable to me, fince
" it gives me a faint refemblance of a
" very eftimable friend."

" I knew," faid Fitzofborne, fixing
his eyes upon her with a moft penetrat-
ing glance, " that your foul was really
" formed for friendfhip. I am a phy-
" fiognomift, madam."

" I do not fufpect you of magical
" fkill," replied Geraldine laughing,
" for I am very much inclined to con-
" trovert your opinion. I never had
" but one intimate friendfhip ; and I
" meet with my Lucy too feldom, and
" our epiftolary communications are too
" limited, to admit of our attachment
" im-

" imprinting any ftrong lines upon my
" countenance; even allowing what I
" am not inclined to admit, that mental
" habits imprefs indelible marks upon
" the mufcular organs."

" I muft enter upon a defence of my
" art, madam; and if I am betrayed
" into any improprieties, remember
" yourfelf only can be to blame. You
" have long been attached to this lady,
" and fhe is fenfible, animated, and pe-
" netrating."

" If you go on with fuch fortunate
" guefles, I fhall begin to retract, and
" believe you poffeffed of the power of
" divination."

" I only wifh to convince you, that
" a conftant perfeverance in one train
" of thought muft give a correct habit
" to the mind, and diffufe a ferene
" dignity over the countenance. And
" certainly the collifion of two ingenuous
" minds

" minds will brighten the qualities of
" each. The foul ever feeks its coun-
" terpart, and tries to affimilate itfelf to
" what it admires. Your correfpondence
" with a perfon fuch as you allow this
" lady to be, accounts for the fparkling
" intelligence of your mannèr, and all
" the lively emanations of your fafcinat-
" ing wit."

The countefs replied with a blufhing
fmile, " I believe you are labouring
" under a little illufion. You certainly
" miftake me for lady Arabella ; or are
" you fo accuftomed to compliment,
" that you involuntarily adopt that ftrain
" to every body ?"

" You may miftake my character,
" madam," faid Fitzofborne ; " but it
" is impoffible that I can fuppofe you
" are lady Arabella." A deep figh
efcaped at thofe words. He hefitated,
and then proceeded : " I can, however,
" entreat

" entreat your pardon with a better
" grace, as I did not feek an opportu-
" nity of expreffing the fentiments
" which I ftrongly feel. If there be
" any indecorum in admiring you and
" requefting your friendfhip, recollect,
" madam, I fhare that guilt with the
" original of this charming portrait."

The countefs immediately replied:
" Every branch of lord Monteith's
" family has indubitable claims on my
" attention. Give me leave to affure
" you, that his lordfhip regards you
" with the fincereft efteem, and that he
" is impatient for an event to take place
" which will cement his friendfhip by
" the bond of alliance."

" If it be in my power to make lady
" Arabella happy——," faid Fitzofborne,
fixing his eyes upon the ground, and
feeming to plunge into a gloomy chaos
of doubt; " but I will hope for the beft.

"We know, that 'whatever is is right.'
"As the world is now conftituted, events
"are not in our own hands." He then
rofe, and took leave with a more profound figh than any he had before uttered. "Poor man!" ejaculated lady
Monteith, "his feelings are too acute
"for happinefs. He will become a
"prey to the moft morbid melancholy,
"and his inattentive wife will confider
"his dejection as a fufficient excufe for
"her diffipation. I fee he is forced
"into this fatal connexion by his friends.
"Why does he not exert the natural in-
"dependence of his energetic character,
"and contemn the mercenary bond?
"How happy would he be with fuch a
"partner as my Lucy!"

Could lady Monteith have penetrated
the dark difguifes of premeditating
villany, how different would have been
the conclufion of her mental foliloquy!

She

She would as foon have pointed out an
alliance between the meek dignified
Octavia, and the infidious, cruel, im-
penetrable Tiberius. And now let me
for a few moments exercife that digref-
five privilege which I have claimed for
moral purpofes.

I would afk the accurate judges of
mankind, what ftriking traits of fuperior
eminence are yet vifible in Fitzofborne's
conduct? what generous fentiment
falling fpontaneoufly from the tongue?
what artlefs difcovery of the genuine
emotions of an upright worthy heart?
Are they charmed with the morals of a
man, whofe ambiguous expreffions can
only be interpreted by fuppofing that he
fecretly defpifes the woman whom he
avowedly purfues? Contempt for fuch
mercenary treachery muft be the natural
fentiment in unfophifticated minds; and
contempt muft rife into abhorrence in

every

every breaſt that is uncorrupted by the laxity of modern principles, if they ſuppoſe that his ardent commendations of a *married* lady were intended to convey to her heart the audacious idea, that they proceeded from the warm emotions of preference.

The mind of Geraldine was unſophiſticated and incorrupt. She ſaw his reluctance to his intended marriage, and interpreted his praiſes as he deſigned ſhe ſhould. Yet neither contempt nor abhorrence aroſe in her breaſt. On the contrary, though ſteadily determined to prevent any inſinuation to lady Arabella's diſadvantage, and to repreſs every expreſſion inconſiſtent with the pure dignity of a matron, ſhe felt for the wiley Fitzoſborne a mixture of pity and eſteem.

——O Flattery !
How ſoon thy ſoft inſinuating oil
Supples the toughest ſouls !

What

What better method can I adopt to convince the younger part of my readers of the neceffity of fhutting their ears to the fyren fong, than placing the example of lady Monteith full in their view? Adorned with every natural and acquired accomplifhment; " chafte as the ificle on Dian's temple ;" attached to her hufband; the fondeft of mothers; domeftic, prudent, and religious. What profanation even to *fuppofe* fuch confummate excellence open to an illicit attack! Yet Fitzofborne, deeply verfed in the fcience of human frailty, no fooner perceived that her vanity liftened to his blandifhments, than he not only determined to *affail* her principles, but felt a firm conviction that his enterprize would *fucceed*.

Her delicacy required, and his duplicity meditated, a covert affault. He perceived on recollection, that he had

been

been too unguarded in the preceding
converfation, and he refolved to follow
the path which fhe had pointed out, by
affecting great refpect for lady Arabella,
and cultivating the friendfhip of lord
Monteith. He defpifed his lordfhip's
abilities too much to fear that his obfervation would be any impediment to his
views; and his own affumption of the
title of a hufband would only give an
unprincipled feducer more unfufpected
opportunities of forwarding his infidious
defigns.

His vifits were now generally made
when he knew that lord Monteith was
at home ; and if his lordfhip was abroad,
he only left a card for the countefs. His
behaviour to her, when they met in
company, was pointedly refpectful and
referved. But care was always taken to
fhow that fuch referve was the effect of
painful effort. By ftudioufly avoiding

every

every opportunity of engaging her in converfation, and by a marked neglect of thofe offices of general civility which the laws of politenefs prefcribed, he appeared fearful of trufting to the fufceptibility of his own heart. He feemed only anxious to guard his mind from the intrufion of every image inconfiftent with his fidelity to lady Arabella. His eyes were fixed upon her, as if he hoped to difcover fomething worthy of his attention. Sometimes, indeed, they wandered to lady Monteith; but if fhe obferved him, they were inftantly withdrawn, with an expreffion of regret for the involuntary dereliction.

His aim was to exhibit a fuperior mind, inflexible in principle, but tenderly fufceptible, maintaining a fevere ftruggle, and determined to be victorious. Lady Monteith was fo far the dupe of his artifices, as to view his conduct

in

in the light that he defired. But fhe alfo drew from it a confequence which he did not intend. She fancied his apparent efforts were fuccefsful, and fhe now only regretted, that Arabella wanted both the inclination and the capacity to improve her delicate fituation to her own advantage.

It has been obferved, that the feducer feveral times conquers his unwarrantable defires in the courfe of his guilty purfuit. Compelled to adopt difguifes, to confult opportunities, to avoid premature difcoveries, the pain of repeated reftrictions, impofed for the purpofes of vice, is greater than would attend the virtuous refolution of abandoning the infidious project. This obfervation was eminently juft in the inftance of Fitzofborne. His foul was not whirled along by the tempeft of paffion. Beauty did not excite violent emotion. Senfe

and

and fweetnefs carried with them no ir-
refiftible charm. His frigid heart was
too cold and felfifh to prompt his diabolical invention, or to extenuate his
crimes. His vices were fyftematic, the
refult of defign, guided by method,
fanctioned by fophiftry, and originating
from the covert war which he waged,
not merely againft the chaftity, but alfo
againft the principles of his victims:
not folely againft their reputation, their
peace of mind, and their temporal profpects, but againft their notions of rectitude and religion, againft thofe immortal
hopes which fuftain the afflicted and
footh the corroding pangs of repentant
guilt.

To lady Arabella, unconfcious of his
defigns, Fitzofborne's increafed attentions gave a livelier pleafure, from the
idea that he intended by that means to

con-

convey a marked contempt of the
countess. Her elation would have been
more complete, if he would have cordially joined in those remarks on the
person and behaviour of Geraldine
which supplied lady Madelina's domestic
party with an agreeable topic for conversation. She recollected, however,
with satisfaction, that if he did not *join*
in these censures, he did not contradict
them, and the extenuating apologies
which he sometimes urged might rather
be termed an attempt to " damn with
faint praise," than a friendly defence. She
was confirmed in her opinion, that her
admirer secretly despised lady Monteith's
pretensions to mental superiority, by ob-
serving, that her *bons mots* and remarks
passed equally unregarded, while her
own were sure of having in him one attentive listener. Lady Arabella's views
of

of life were neither very accurate nor extenſive. Yet ſhe had ſome ſuſpicion that the connubial bond operated as a powerful ſoporific upon the deference, obſervance, and tenderneſs, which lovers ſometimes, even in this refined age, think proper to aſſume. Her dear viſcounteſs had aſſured her, that if Edward's behaviour as a huſband equalled his attentions as an admirer, they would certainly be pointed at as an *exemplary* couple ; for that at preſent all the world knew him by the title of lady Arabella Macdonald's ſlave. No one more ſtrongly felt thoſe paſſions which Pope affirms to be the predominate features in the mind of women, " the love of pleaſure" and " the love of ſway," than her ladyſhip. But ſince it was at leaſt doubtful, whether ſhe could continue to be " queen for life," ſhe was deſirous to protract the period which acknow-

ledged

ledged her right of government; and, as the gentleman, was not very urgent for an early day, the lady's fenfibility was not hurt by repeated denials.

Another unexpected caufe of delay at this time intervened. Lady Madelina had often declared, that as foon as fhe had fettled her dear niece to her fatif-faction, fhe fhould have entirely done with a world of which fhe repeatedly affured her friends fhe was quite weary. Twenty years before, on her firft mar-riage with her ever-lamented fir Simon Frazer, fhe had ufed fimilar expreffions. She then faid that fhe only lived for his fake; and if fhe were fo unfortunate as to lofe him, her " occupation would be gone," and exiftence would become an infupportable burden. But as that de-precated event did happen without any lafting change in her ladyfhip's apparent relifh for the good things of this life, it
                                        was

was fufpected, that twenty years hence her affectionate heart might find fome pretext for that ftrong attachment to her perfon, which her exceffive attention to her own health and fafety rendered vifible to all who knew her. When the reader, therefore, confiders the infinite fucceffion of laft plans, and final engagements, which fhe would probably have pleaded, his fenfibility will be lefs hurt to find, that death dealt by her, as he did by " the fair lady in coftly robes," mentioned in the good old fong, by compelling her to truft future events to that Providence whofe fuperintendence had not been her favourite fpeculation.

I have obferved, that the fettlements were drawn up under lady Madelina's eye, who feemed defirous of extending the fupremacy which fhe had uniformly exercifed over every perfon with whom fhe was connected (except her niece) beyond

beyond the grave. She had multiplied
entails, and confidered every poffible
event of contention, feparation, divorce,
and fecond marriage. She had explored
the family pedigree, picked out the
moft fonorous hereditary chriftian names,
and ftringing three or four together,
which were capable of liquid pronunciation, fhe ordered, that they fhould be
adopted by the fucceffive fons and
daughters of this intended marriage, on
pain of forfeiting all right to inheritance.
Jointure, pin-money, and alimony took
up feveral pages, and the finifhed deed
had more the appearance of a truce
between two inveterate enemies than a
recognition of mutual confidence and
efteem. The very fight of thefe for-
midable parchments muft have annihilated the whole court of Cytherea; but
fortunately the modern Hymen never
brings his caufes before that tribunal,
which

which is now exclufively employed in trying affairs of libertinifm, or, as it is politely termed, gallantry.

Lady Madelina perufed the ftupendous performance with delight; weighed the technical meaning of every word which the ufeful tautology of the law had introduced; and, trufting that the united names of Fitzofborne, Frazer, and Macdonald might found in courts and caftles a thoufand years hence, declared that fhe was *perfectly fatisfied.* It is fuppofed, that the pronunciation of thofe words, which fhe had never before been known to ufe, occafioned a mortal revulfion in her oracular organs, for fhe was found fpeechlefs next morning. Lady Arabella's determined refolution of enjoying the pleafures of a public breakfaft prevented her from attending to the affurances of her aunt's woman, that fuch a change muft be inevitably

followed

followed by mortal consequences. She
contented herself with leaving positive
orders to be immediately sent for if lady
Madelina grew worse, and drove off
with lady Fitzosborne, who convinced
her that she was perfectly right; for,
as the patient could not speak, company
could do her no service. The office of
smoothing the bed of death devolved
on Geraldine, who hastened to the
house of mourning at the first intimation of what had happened, and arrived
a few moments before lady Madelina
expired.

CHAP. XXVI.

Let then the fair one beautifully cry,
In Magdalene's loose hair and lifted eye.

POPE.

THE melancholy event related in my laſt Chapter was ſpeedily conveyed to the gay groupe whom the elegant *dejeuné* of the ducheſs of A. had aſſembled on the flowery banks of Thames. It was announced to lady Arabella with very little preparation; for as, in compliance with the wiſhes of the company, though declaredly out of ſpirits, ſhe had juſt conſented to exhibit her own fine perſon and her lover's to the beſt advantage by ſtanding up in a reel, no one ſuppoſed but that ſhe might hear the ſad tale with decent compoſure. It was, however, quite
the

the reverſe, and her ſenſibility now became as remarkable, as her fortitude
had been before. She fainted, fell into
hyſterics, wept, recovered, and was at
laſt conveyed apparently lifeleſs to her
carriage. Every creature preſent par-
took in her concern for lady Madelina's
death, for it certainly ſpoiled a moſt
delightful party. Though the company
endeavoured to recover their ſpirits
after the fair mourner was removed, all
attempts at brilliancy was prevented by
the unavoidable intruſion of ſerious ideas.
The ladies grew as ſtupid as if they were
at church. Death's heads and phyſicians
intruded into every ſubject ; and the laſt
topic of converſation that was ſtarted by
the gentlemen was a diſcuſſion of the
merits of the patent coffin.

Lady Arabella was accompanied
home by the Fitzoſbornes. The viſcounteſs engaged in the friendly taſk
of

of confolation, while Edward, leaning
back with his arms folded, and his eyes
fixed upon the lovely fufferer, (I fuppofe)
more deeply fympathized in her forrow;
for the harangues of the comforter were
only interrupted by lady Arabella's fobs
and fighs, which did not abate in violence, though lady Fitzofborne was diffufe on the folly of grieving for what
was fure to happen, and therefore what
nobody could prevent. The carriage
at length ftopped. Lady Arabella was
fupported up ftairs, fwallowed more
hartfhorn, and at length became fufficiently compofed to make inquiries
after the particulars of an event of
which fhe had only yet received a
general account.

Lady Madelina's firft gentlewoman,
a Macdonald by an indirect defcent,
entered on the fad recital. Nothing
could be more capable of being com-
preffed

preffed into a fmall compafs; but Mrs.
Margaret was eminently gifted with
that fpecies of oratory which may be
termed expanfion. Her poor dear lady's
merits, her poor dear lady's fufferings,
the confidence her poor dear lady placed
in her faithful fervices, and a firm conviction, that fhe never fhould furvive
her poor dear lady: thefe topics were
expatiated upon, till Arabella became a
little difpleafed, that any one fhould take
up grief juft at the inftant herfelf had
laid it down. It came out in the courfe
of the narration, that from fome peculiar
circumftances lady Monteith had adopted an opinion, that the fpark of life
was not actually extinguifhed; but that
the fpeedy exertion of proper means
might revive the fufpended animation.
To this opinion the phyficians, who
had been fummoned, lent fome countenance; and the humanity of the
countefs

countefs prompted her not only to com-
mand thefe applications, but by her
prefence to prevent the proceedings
which are fometimes injudicioufly
adopted at the firft moment of apparent
diffolution.

Mrs. Margaret was not only convinced of the inefficacy of the attempt,
but, confcientioufly believing it to be
very prefumptuous, had refufed her
fervices, with fome little fenfe of indig-
nity at having had them required, and
keen fufceptibility at the fuppofition
that fhe could bear to ftay in the room
where her poor dear lady lay. Arabella
joined in her opinion; and the difcourfe
changed from the virtues of Mrs.
Margaret and the deceafed, to the
wickednefs of difturbing the dead, and
the concern which the affectionate niece
now felt, that her dear aunt had none of

her

her *own* family to attend her in her laſt moments.

The failure of lady Monteith's efforts relieved Arabella from what might more properly be called a vexation than a diſtreſs; and her ſofter feelings, freed from diſagreeable embarraſſments, had leiſure to flow in the delicate channels which etiquette preſcribes to grief. She mourned for one fortnight in the ſweeteſt manner imaginable, dreſſed in a cloſe cap with her bouquet ſtuck on one ſide, her robe looſely faſtened, and her arms hanging negligently. All her viſitants agreed, that ſhe looked prettier than ever, and Fitzoſborne was continually reminded of thoſe well-known lines which characterize the fair ſex, as deſigned to " be adorned by diſtreſs," and " dreſſed moſt amiably in tears."

But

But it was not over the unconscious tomb that this fair flowret drooped. The increased sensibility of the present age, grown too fragile to encounter the morbid contagion of death, declines all intimate acquaintance with spectacles of mortality, and deputes hireling hands to perform those offices which the sterner fortitude of former times claimed as the peculiar privilege of affection and kindred. My attachment to obsolete manners inclines me to refer the universal custom of flying from the bed of death and its melancholy appendages, to some other cause than excessive tenderness. I suspect the fastidiousness of indulgence, accustomed to bask in the sunshine of life, and bereft of sufficient energy even to wish to procure a defence against the storm. I discover the enervating habits of dissipation, the cant of flattery, and the sophisms of self-delusion.

lufion. Beauty will not contemplate the fixed raylefs eye, left the recollection fhould obfcure the brilliancy of its own : youth and health refufe to be acquainted with the livid cheek, which preaches the importance of the paffing hours ; and gaiety abjures all knowledge of the clay-cold reliques of the human form, left the fearful fentence of " fuch fhalt thou be" fhould palfy the graceful ftep, arreft the fwift career of levity, and render the whifper of adulation unin-terefting.

Lady Arabella's firft tears flowed be-neath her brother's roof; but her ex-treme fufceptibility foon required a frefh afylum. Lady Monteith was the worft comforter in the world; and fhe was convinced that her poor fpirits would be quite overcome, if fhe did not get amongft people a little more like other folks. Geraldine indeed had performed

the

the office of a confoler to her Lucy with
tolerable fuccefs; but the retired daughter of a country clergyman, and a fafhionable belle, are different characters:
and either the fimplicity of the countefs
did not difcriminate, or fome fecret
fpark of ill-nature prevented her from
adopting the proper method of treating
her prefent gueft. She permitted lady
Arabella's tears to ftream without any
admonition that they might dim her
eyes or injure her complexion; and
in the moft violent paroxyfms of grief
fhe ftrove to foften her emotions by
leading the difcourfe to her dear aunt's
affection for her, and anxious folicitude
to promote her happinefs. She had
once the inhumanity to fuggeft the idea,
that the feparated fpirit would be afflicted
by witneffing the forrow of furviving
friends; and that the violent indulgence
of extreme regret might be conftrued

to proceed from a want of due fubmiffion
to the Supreme Difpofer of events. She
had indeed fuccefsfully expatiated on
thefe topics to Mifs Evans. The
countenance of that artlefs girl affumed
an angelic compofure whilft liftening
to the folemn fentiments; and her hands
and eyes uplifted in meek refignation
feemed to fay, " I will not impede the
" beatitude of my mother, nor murmur
" at the difpenfations of my God."

But in the prefent inftance the awful
allufion produced very horrific effects.
Lady Arabella's ideas of "things unfeen"
were extremely confufed. She had never
had time to inveftigate the fubject herfelf; and, from fome arguments which
Mr. Fitzofborne had ufed, fhe was inclined to hope, that the vague notions
which fhe had picked up in her early
years were purely chimerical terrors,
the effect of low prejudices. She, therefore,

fore, replied to the confolatory arguments of the countefs with a fhriek of
apprehenfion; befought her in future to
avoid fuch fhocking expreffions; and,
looking round her, as if in expectation
of feeing lady Madelina's ghoft, fhe
became fo fearful of having a vifionary
attendant, that fhe durft not move from
one room to another without being accompanied by a corporeal guard.

At Mr. Fitzofborne's next vifit fhe
expatiated on the premeditated cruelty
of lady Monteith, who chofe the very
period of her being fo low that fhe could
hardly fupport herfelf, to afflict her by
naming fubjects that fhe never could
bear. She was perfectly innocent, fhe
faid; had never hurt any body, nor
committed any crime in her life; and
why need fhe be talked to about feparated fpirits, and religion, as if fhe were
the greateft finner in the world? Lady

Monteith

Monteith had even hinted, that there would be an indecorum in her going into public immediately after the interment of an aunt, who had to her fupplied the tendernefs and protection of the maternal character; and fhe was certain that the funeral was delayed, not fo much out of refpect, as to keep her immured, and to make her break her heart, which was much too refined and tender to endure thofe forms of woe to which ftronger minds might fubmit. In fine, fhe enjoined Fitzofborne to ftate to lady Monteith the impropriety of her conduct, and to convince her how wrong it was to talk about difagreeable things which fhe could not be fure were true. Edward undertook the office, but advifed lady Arabella not to be too fanguine of fuccefs. Prejudices, he faid, were ftubborn things to contend with, and lady Monteith had unfortunately imbibed feveral.

feveral. He complimented lady Arabella on her more enlarged notions, but conjured her to conceal a fuperiority which might probably excite envy; and in cafe of any future attempts to infpire her with fuperftitious terrors, he wifhed her either to give a fudden turn to the converfation, or to enjoy the triumph of reafon over bigotry in a dignified filence.

Fitzofborne entered on the tafk enjoined, with the cruel avidity of a fanguinary mind, bent on deftroying what it was neceffitated to revere. His obfervations on lady Monteith's behaviour enabled him clearly to develope her character; and as he founded his hopes of fuccefs on her evident love of praife, he was fenfible that the unaffected fincerity of her religious principles would prove a fteady bulwark too powerful to be affailed by open attacks, and which he muft either undermine or abandon

I 3   his

his purfuit.   He perceived, that though
her vivacity at times tranfcended the
limits of rigid prudence, even in the
wildeft flights of gaiety the moft guarded
ridicule on facred fubjects was unpalat-
able ; and though the engroffing amufements of polite life afforded lefs leifure
for reflection and devotional exercifes
during her ftay in town, fhe ever paffed a
diffipated Sunday with evident regret, and
appeared to feel every omiffion of duty
with the felf-reproach of confcious error,
rather than to avow her neglect with the
bold air of one who expects to be applauded for liberality and exemption
from prefcribed forms.   The footing on
which he was received in the family gave
him frequent occafions of perceiving
that, though fhe did not burft out into
frequent cenfures againft licentioufnefs,
fhe never treated a grofs deviation from
morality and decorum with that levity
                                        of

of remark which warrants the conclusion, that the obferver's principles are
too relaxed to view flagitious conduct
with proper abhorrence. Though no
one knew better how to wing the fhaft
of raillery, and to encourage "sport
that wrinkled care derides," wit was
with her the companion of unreproved
pleafure, not the child of unreftrained
liberty. Its frolic hand was ever taught
to refpect the palladium of virtue and
religion.

The event which Geraldine had lately
witneffed confirmed her habitual reverence for ferious fubjects. Without pro-
feffing to feel any marked attachment to
lady Madelina, or affecting forrow for
her lofs, fhe had contemplated an object of mortality with the fympathetic
thoughtfulnefs of one who felt confcious
that fhe was a fellow-pilgrim, journeying

to

to the same bourne. A conviction of the inftability of temporal poffeffions, and the inefficiency of human aid, would naturally direct a confiderate mind to firmer fupports, and to recur to the idea of a traveller, than which nothing can be more analogous to human life. The certainty of a limited refidence amongft the objects of fenfe excited a ftrong folicitude to extend her knowledge of things invifible, and to fecure an intereft in that undifcovered world of which fhe muft one day become an inhabitant.

A ftate of mind like that which I have defcribed appears at the firft glance to be unfavourable to the defigns of a Fitzofborne. He thought it otherwife. It was a difpofition which naturally led to the difcuffion of moral and religious truths. The decent forms which the cuftom of the world ftill fanctions pre-
                                    fcribed

fcribed to the Monteiths the neceffity of avoiding promifcuous vifitors, and abfenting from public amufements. And though the fair Arabella feemed to caft a longing look from her folitude upon forbidden pleafure, the countefs liftened to the narrative of the day with a more languid attention, and imperceptibly led back the converfation to fome improving fubjeft. Her attempts generally frightened lady Arabella, and compelled her to take refuge in her own apartments; where fhe found occupation in confulting with her maid on the changes of ornament which the alterations in her mourning would admit. Lord Monteith, though at firft doubtful how he fhould kill time during this melancholy period of confinement, found fo much amufement in ringing the dumb bell and learning to play on the violin, that he re-

lapfed

lapfed into his old misfortune of want of leifure; and Fitzofborne would have found it more difficult to avoid than to felect opportunities for private converfation with Geraldine.

CHAP. XXVII.

—— In difcourfe more fweet——
Others apart fat on a hill retir'd,
In thoughts more elevate, and reafon'd high
Of Providence, fore-knowledge, will, and fate,
Fix'd fate, free will, fore-knowledge abfolute,
And found no end, in wandering mazes loft.
Of good and evil much they argued, then,
Of happinefs and final mifery,
Paffion and apathy, glory and fhame,
Vain wifdom all, and falfe philofophy.

MILTON.

READING was one of lady Monteith's conftant amufements; and among her favourite writers the moral pages of Johnfon held a diftinguifhed pre-eminence. His inftructive romance of Raffelas occupied her one morning. She ftopped at the part which feemed to intimate the author's belief in the poffibility of fpectral appearances. The idea ftrongly engroffed her imagination. She

rumi-

ruminated on the arguments which might be adduced on either fide, and continued in a profound reverie when Fitzofborne entered the room.

After a paufe, in which lady Monteith was trying to difengage her ideas from the train of reflection which they had purfued, Edward politely expreffed his fears that he had interrupted an agreeable ftudy; and, with an intimation that he would immediately withdraw, inquired what fubject occupied her attention. She delivered to him the unclofed volume without any comment. He read the paffage to which her finger referred, and reftored it with an obfervation, that the Britifh cenfor was perfectly confiftent. Geraldine, miftaking this remark for approbation, replied, that fhe had ever thought him fo, and therefore ftrove to form her mind by the exalted ftandard his works prefcribed.

"I agree

" I agree with you," said Fitzofborne.
" His writings do indeed prefcribe an
" exalted ftandard of morality. A gi-
" gantic one, I fhould rather fay, utterly
" inadequate to the prefent ftate of the
" world. His views and writings are,
" however, all uniform. An enemy to
" levity and fimplicity, a lover of difci-
" pline and fyftem, averfe to thofe rights
" which man inherently poffeffes, tena-
" cious of thofe bulwarks which fociety
" forms, he is repulfive in his politics,
" uncomplying in his morality, and
" auftere in his religion."

It was only the laft obfervation which
convinced the countefs that this exordium was defigned to cenfure her favourite author, and fhe began his defence by making fome preliminary conceffions. In extenuation of that air of
difcontent and depreffion which ever
pervades his works when he refers to
the

the fituation of a profeffed writer, fhe
maintained that large allowances ought
to be made for the fenfibility of unpa-
tronized merit, confcious of defert and
ftruggling under calamity. She added,
that the fituation of the moralift in his
early years precluded him from entering
into thofe more refined claffes of fociety,
whofe amiable polifh might have foftened the afperities of his natural character. But fince the world already
poffeffed many elegant inftructors, who
knew how to aim the lighter fhafts of
fatire, and to blend improvement with
amufement, perhaps the lover of litera-
ture would not regret the circumftances
that gave him one lefs urbane moralift,
whofe auftere fenfe exhibited the nobleft
model of energetic compofition and exalted principle.

"Your juftification, madam," faid
Fitzofborne, "is conclufive. The page
"of

" of Johnson will ever be reforted to by
" the lover of variety, and will claim
" the appropriate commendations which
" you have given it, from minds capa-
" ble of appreciating his real worth.
" He is too profound to be the idol of
" the million : and as his beauties can
" only be relifhed by an underftanding
" as vigorous as his own, fo his precepts
" feem calculated for difpofitions that
" refemble him in firmnefs.   On fuch
" ftrong minds his tendency to fuper-
" ftition can produce no bad effects."

" My acquaintance is too limited,"
rejoined the countefs, " for me to know
" a perfon to whom I could not fafely
" recommend the works of Johnfon."

" I beg your pardon," interrupted
Edward.   " I fhould have many objec-
" tions to lady Arabella's feeing the
" paffage which has wrought your mind
" into its prefent ftate of *high* enthufiafm.
                                    " The

" The uncommon fufceptibility and
" delicacy of her character would make
" her feel painful alarms, while I fee
" you only indulge a ' fine frenzy.' In
" a converfation you lately had with.
" her, even fome of your guarded ex-
" preffions have caufed her the moft
" diftreffing agitation."

Lady Monteith recollected that fhe
was talking to a lover, and determined
to endure a little puerility. She acknowledged, that it was natural for
Arabella to feem depreffed immediately
after the lofs of a friend who had acted
the part of a fofter-mother to her, and
fhe promifed to be very cautious in future. " But," continued fhe, " I muft
" own that the invifible agency of fe-
" parated fpirits is a very favourite theme
" with me; and though, contrary to
" the opinion of the Abyffinian fage, I
" could affirm, that we never have any

7   " certain

" certain evidence that the dead are
" permitted to become objects of our
" senses, I have long rejoiced in the
" hope that our departed friends are
" the agents employed by over-ruling
" Providence to perform offices of care
" and tenderness to their surviving com-
" nexions. This thought has most fre-
" quently occurred to me, as I have
" bent over my sleeping children, and I
" have fancied glorified beings watched
" our unconscious hours with similar
" attention. When I was once threat-
" ened with the loss of my eldest darling,
" I found sensible consolation in the idea
" of its becoming a guardian cherub to
" sustain the innocence of its sisters
" through a dangerous world, and to
" receive my parting spirit at the hour
" of my dissolution."

While the countess spoke, her radiant
eyes were suffused with tears. Fitzofborne,

borne, checking fome unfubdued ftrug-
gles of confcience, which almoft tempted
him to wifh he could enjoy fuch vifionary
delights, coolly replied to her energetic
fpeech : " I fhould be very forry, ma-
" dam, to interrupt thofe agreeable re-
" veries which in minds of your tem-
" perature can *rarely* be prejudicial.   I
" fhall only ftate the dangerous confe-
" quences of fuch illufions becoming
" general.   What a tremendous fuper-
" ftructure of impofition might prieft-
" craft erect upon fuch a vifionary bafis!
" You do not pretend, madam, to fay,
" that your hopes reft upon any real
" foundation. The nature of the foul
" has hitherto eluded inquiry. It may
" in time become capable of abfolute
" definition ; and though the age is not
" at prefent fufficiently enlightened to
" afford abfolute proof of this fuppofed
" immaterial fubftance being only a
                              " more

" more exquifité configuration of perifh-
" able atoms, incàpable of diftinct exift-
" ence, the glorious epocha of truth and
" reafon is too near to allow us to believe
" the poffibility of fpectral appearances,
" or even of fpiritual agency, in the
" manner your imagination prompts you
" to wifh."

Though lady Monteith was no deep
theologian, fhe had heard of the mille-
nium, and the fufpenfion of confcioufnefs
in the difembodied foul; and fhe concluded that Fitzofborne was a convert
to thofe doctrines. She was by no means
aware of the deeper tendency of his
views; yet, as fhe thought there was
fomething peculiar in his opinions, fhe
wifhed to fathom him upon thefe fubjects. She knew enough of the world
to be convinced, that divinity was not
the favourite ftudy of young men of fafhion; but fhe knew too, that deep

learning

learning was equally excluded from polite
circles. Fitzofborne had been announced
to her as the " mirror of information ;"
and fhe faw nothing ridiculous in the
idea, that a man of reading fhould devote a part of his attention to the ftudy
of the nobleft truths.   Indifference on
ferious fubjects was, as far as her obfervations extended, combined with ignorance and a general relaxation of mind.
Fitzofborne's manner evinced energy and
attention.   She had often felt indignant
at hearing the witling attempt to ridicule
what he did not underftand, or the libertine feek to invalidate what he feared
to believe.   But Fitzofborne poffeffed
too much real talent to envy the wreath
that fades upon the coxcomb's brow,
and his conduct feemed too correct to
fupply him with a motive for taking
fhelter in infidelity.   His fentiments on
every fubject were moral and liberal.
                                           His

His felf-command was exemplary; his information general; his reafoning, though flowery, ingenious, and, in lady Monteith's opinion, judicious. I have already obferved, that her parts were rather brilliant than profound. It will not therefore be furprifing, that fhe fhould be eafily entangled in the fnare of a fyllogifm, or that the unfufpecting fincerity of her heart fhould render her a dupe to any one who took the trouble to play the fpecious confummate hypocrite.

In forming her opinion of the dangerous character which was now expofed to her obfervation, fhe had fallen into the fame error of precipitate judgment which fhe had been guilty of in the cafe of lord Monteith. She now fupplied talents with as much liberality as fhe formerly created virtues. Experience had convinced her, that love is

apt

apt to look through magnifying optics ;
yet, though one pleafing phantom faded
after another, fomething really eftimable
ftill remained ; and on her comparing
her own lot with that of others, fhe
found abundant reafon to acquiefce in a
ftate of refigned content. Recalling
fome of Mrs. Evans's early precepts, fhe
had laboured to fubdue thofe more exquifite refinements of fenfibility, which
vainly look for confummate enjoyment
in this world ; and, without feeling too
lively regrets for the want of unattainable
good, fhe enjoyed the cup of blefling
which Providence tendered to her ac-
ceptance.   She was in this ftate of mind
when her acquaintance with Fitzofborne
commenced.   The peculiarity of his
character drew her attention.   The evident infelicity of his connubial profpects
attracted pity.   His conduct awakened
efteem, and his intellectual fuperiority
excited

excited admiration. Neither did fhe difcover from what fecret failing in herfelf
that admiration fprung, nor that Vanity
is as great a magnifier as Love.

Fitzofborne had been fo careful to
veil his fcepticifm in ambiguous phrafes,
that lady Monteith's folicitude to difcover his principles really arofe from an
idea that their fingularity chiefly proceeded from their excellence, and that
by converfing with him fhe fhould
ftrengthen her own convictions. She
had often lamented, that lord Monteith's
volatile temper deprived her of that fup-
porting judgment and directing care
which the conjugal inftitution was intended to afford to the fofter fex.
Though not doubtful of the propriety
of her own conduct, fhe naturally wifhed
it fhould receive the approbation of an
obferving eye ; and a confcioufnefs of
her own abilities was attended with fome
repugnance

repugnance to their " wafting their
fweetnefs in the defert air." The friend,
the advifer fhe had long wifhed for,
feemed now to prefent himfelf to her
view in the perfon of an accomplifhed
intelligent gentleman of irreproachable
worth, who would foon become a near
relation. Every idea of impropriety was
removed by this latter confideration;
and, with the ufual imbecility of fhort-
fighted mortals, fhe fancied her character might acquire additional luftre by
imbibing the fplendor of fo fair an arche-
type. She had not difcovered, that

All was falfe, and hollow; though his tongue
Dropp'd manna, and could make the worfe appear
The better reafon, to perplex and dafh
Matureft councils; for his thoughts were low;
To vice induftrious, but to nobler deeds
Tim'rous and flothful; yet he pleas'd the ear.

Her endeavours to diveft this " Demon
of fentiment" of his cherubic veil
were

were, however ineffectual. Wrapped in his darling myſticiſm, he defied her ſcrutiny. His knowledge of the human heart convinced him how powerful an engine ſecreſy becomes when wielded by a ſkilful hand, and oppoſed to the reſtleſs ſpirit of female curioſity. But while he eluded her inquiries, and avoided a full diſcovery of his own opinions, he threw out enough to convince her, that they were not only extraordinary but permanent; and by complimenting the ſagacious avidity with which ſhe ſeized every ſentiment he ſeemed unwarily to diſcloſe, he rouſed the mingled ſolicitude of inquiſitiveneſs and vanity, and formed an intereſt which he determined to improve.

The converſation ended on his part with a panegyric on morality, which he loaded with oſtentatious ornaments; and a philippic againſt the illiberality of ſuppoſ-

ing

ing that exalted minds needed any other inducement to act rightly than the abstract loveliness of virtue. His last observation was prefaced by a solemn avowal of his own respect for religion, which he acknowledged to be a most useful invention, and a necessary restriction upon the untutored part of mankind. He left lady Monteith in a sort of maze, regretting that he had not been more explicit on those points in which he had confessed his opinions differed from hers, delighted with his pure morality, and enchanted with his conversation.

Her reverie was interrupted by lady Arabella's requesting the favour of her opinion, whether tiffany jessamine, or crape roses, would make the most elegant festoon. She listened with perplexed attention to a recapitulation of the light airiness of the former ornament, and the quiet accommodation of the

12   latter;

latter; and she felt mortified at being obliged to witness the effect of their alternate display on her ladyship's court dress. While her eyes were fixed upon vacancy, and her thoughts were regreting the wilful negligence, which would give to Fitzosborne a frivolous unintelligent partner, she, with the indifference of Swift's Vanessa, pronounced an unconscious preference of the crape roses. This fiat was decisive, and lady Arabella returned to her own apartment with her maid and her milliner; a happy groupe, till the discovery, that a lady whom lady Arabella hated wore crape roses, drew from the distressed fair one several pathetic ejaculations on the peculiar unhappiness of her own lot, in being thus prevented from having the prettiest trimming in the world. Some tender tears were dropped, which were placed to the account of her aunt; and after a

few

few expreffions, which from a perfon of
lefs delicacy might be termed fcolding,
fhe difmiffed her terrified auditors with
a declaration that fhe was very low,
and could not bear contradiction and
difappointment.

Meantime lady Monteith had refumed
her ftudies, and began to difcover fome
of thofe faults in her beloved Johnfon
which Fitzofborne had pointed out, when
lord Monteith entered the room, highly
elated that he had juft made himfelf
complete mafter of "Britons ftrike
"home," and entreating her to accompany him upon the harp. She complied; but the fmile of acquiefcence was
more of the penfive than of the exhilarating kind; and her thoughts wandered to the prohibited haunts of ufelefs
regrets for the paft, and vain anticipa-
tions of the future. But while, in her
career of impoffibilities, fhe was begin-
ning

ning to wish that Monteith possessed the
intelligent mind of Fitzosborne, her care-
less hand struck a false chord, and a mechanical impulse aroused her attention
time enough to answer her lord's inquiries, if she was well, and if any thing
made her unhappy. His affectionate
solicitude restored her mind to its usual
temperament, and she chided herself
for indulging a thought inconsistent with
the gratitude and esteem which she
owed to her plighted consort. She recollected, that different excellencies belong to different characters; and that it
is the abuse, not the want, of a talent
which stamps criminality upon any one.
She made allowances for the force of
habit conspiring with strong passions,
unrestrained by an expensive, yet de-
fective, education, and inflamed by the
seductions of affluence and uncontrolled
freedom of action. While these reflec-

K 3   tions

tions fucceffively occupied her mind, a tender fweetnefs diffufed itfelf over her countenance, and her hand executed "Britons ftrike home" entirely to his lordfhip's fatisfaction.

CHAP. XXVII.

Then gay ideas crowd the vacant brain,
While peers and dukes, and all their sweeping train,
And garters, stars, and coronets appear,
And in soft sounds, "Your Grace" salutes the ear.
POPE.

FITZOSBORNE's thoughts were now so engrossed by his intended attack on the principles and honour of lady Monteith, that he felt as little interested about the event of his engagements with lady Arabella as if the marriage ceremony had really taken place. He was roused from this insensibility by the noble viscount his brother, who, having procured a copy of the redoubtable settlement, which I have before mentioned, swore upon his honour (his lordship, though very fond of this oath, was never known to be forsworn) that the terms were too ha

K 4 for

for any man above a fhoe-black to abide
by. " I would have you by all means,
" Ned," faid he, " make a better bar-
" gain for yourfelf. The girl is im-
" menfely fond of you, that is evident;
" and a fellow with a tenth part of your
" addrefs would make the pretty dri-
" veller accede to any thing. Can't
" you give her a little fentiment upon
" the occafion, and tell her, that by re-
" ferving all her fortune in her own
" power, it will be abfolutely impoffible
" for her ever to enjoy the fublime
" gratification of receiving obligations
" from the perfon fhe loves? Can't you
" flourifh too upon the provifion in cafe
" of feparation and divorce, and declare
" that the frigorific idea petrifies your
" whole frame? Be mafter of her fortune,
" however, at all events; for let me
" tell you, my dear lad, a wife's affec-
" tions in this age are but a transferable
" com-

" commodity of little permanent value,
" I assure you."

Edward felt too well convinced of his
influence to doubt the possibility of his
acquiring the glittering prize upon his
own terms; and he sketched in his
mind the only conditions upon which he
would consent to give the lady the honour of his name. These conditions
were remarkable for nothing but their
being a direct contradiction to lady Madelina's plan. But on his first conversation with lady Arabella upon the subject
he discovered, that he had greatly mis-
taken her character when he attributed
to it any degree of pliability in pecuniary
matters. She, indeed, loved to squan-
der with thoughtless profusion; but that
very love of squandering suggested the
propriety of retaining the power of
doing so; and the lovers parted with
great mutual dissatisfaction: Edward

K 5   convinced

convinced that his merits would confer
honour upon any lady on whom he bestowed his hand, and lady Arabella per-
suaded that a younger brother has no
right to expect a higher office than to
be his wife's steward, if he be so lucky
as to engage the good opinion of a
woman of fortune. Both seemed inclined to bring their matrimonial pretensions to a fresh market. He thought
that his person might attract some fair
one equally rich and less mercenary;
and she knew, that when people calcu-
late upon good matches, there is always
as great a difference between present
possession and reversionary expectation,
as there is between the comparative
splendor of a baronial and a ducal coronet. The gentleman pondered upon
the propriety of discontinuing his addresses; but the lady hastened his deli-
berations by informing him, that if his

visits

vifits at Portland-place were upon her account, fhe begged fhe might not in future interrupt his impórtant avoca-tions; and thus Mr. Fitzofborne was fuddenly reduced to the fituation of a *rejeffed* fwain, a condition which the verfatility of his talents knew how to improve.

Lady Arabella's frivolity, felfifhnefs, and avowed expeftation of making fu-perior conquefts, did not difcredit the tale which Fitzofborne told of his dif-miffion. The blunt integrity of lord Monteith's charafter took fire at his fifter's evident dereliftion of the princi-ples of honour, conftancy, and female delicacy; and the reluftance with which the fpecious Edward appeared to difco-ver her caprice irritated his ardent tem-per ftill more. He charged her with bafe infidelity and grofs indecorum; and fhe evaded the charge by urging,

K 6   that

that fhe was a free independent being, and accountable to no one for her actions, which were the refult of her opinions; and no one had any right to fcrutinize the opinions of others. The earl raved againft this heterodox doctrine, becaufe it militated againft his wifh of fupremacy, without difcovering that there was a degree of ingratitude in the application of thefe principles againft the intereft of the mafter from whom fhe had acquired them; and her ladyfhip refolved never to miflead her hufband by furnifhing a previous inftance of her fubmiffion to her brother's authority. She removed on the very evening of the difpute to the houfe of lord vifcount Fitzofborne.

In order to explain the reafon of her choofing that afylum, I muft unriddle a little Machiavelian policy. The fituation of the noble houfe of Fitzofborne was become

become fo very precarious in point of credit, that the reprefentative of its honours, like Shakefpeare's Percy, had long " caft many a northern look to fee the Frazer bring up his powers." The illuftrious vifcount indeed could not give himfelf a legal title to that fpacious inheritance which now centered in lady Arabella; but his fraternal wifh of tranf-ferring it to his own family was not quite difinterefted. Edward had ever ap-peared too abftracted, too generous, and too fuperior to low mercenary views, to deny a brother the loan of a few thoufands, and his indifference to money was in the vifcount's opinion the caufe of his prefent difappointment; for had his whole heart been engroffed by the defire of advancing his fortune, the pretty bird might have beat her gay plumage in ufelefs vexation, at finding

herfelf

herself surrounded by too many toils
ever to hope for recovered liberty.

In opposition to those saturnine cen-
sors who affirm that a genteel pair never
think or act in concert, I have to relate
a scheme in which the viscount and his
lady cordially co-operated, and which,
though it might not terminate in an in-
vocation of Venus's antique doves, promised to produce a modern pigeon.
The farce commenced with a visit from
the viscountess to her dear friend; during
which she heard with mingled surprize
and grief that Mr. Fitzosborne's expectations were so very illiberal, and
his temper so very uncomplying, that
the connection was dissolved. She com-
mended the laudable spirit which dictated lady Arabella's resolution of sooner
breaking her heart than submitting to
unjustifiable demands; but when she
                                    added,

added, that, by thus acting with proper
regard to female dignity, she had excited the resentment of her brother, the
indignation of her sympathizing friend
exceeded all bounds. With bitter sar-
casms on the indelicacy of lord Monteith's interference, she intreated her to
remove directly to lord Fitzofborne's,
and assured her, that offended beauty
would find a protector in the viscount,
who would either compel Edward to
make proper concessions, or disown him
for a brother. There was something
truly *Roman* in this sentiment. It was
expressed with becoming dignity; and
the viscountess, still farther to enforce
it, added, " You will get a little more
" into the world, my dear, from which,
" it is certain, you have lately been too
" much secluded. We have frequently
" little private parties, at which you
" cannot object to taking a card, for
                              " nobody

" nobody will know any thing about it,
" fo that there cannot be any indeco-
" rum. I proteft, I think you grow
" more bewitching every hour. Your
" mourning becomes you fo exquifitely,
" that in pity to the world I ought to
" propofe keeping you fhut up, that
" other belles may have a little chance;
" but I own I am malicious enough to
" wifh to give a little fillip to Edward's
" fears. Nothing is fo animating as a
" ftrong fit of jealoufy, and I know that
" to make frefh conquefts you need
" only appear." So friendfhip urged;
and its arguments were conclufive.

The parties might now be faid to be
fairly drawn up in battle array; for, not
to yield to the Fitzofbornes in hofpita-
lity, lord Monteith had infifted that Edward fhould become his gueft; and,
though their taftes and difpofitions were
by no means in unifon, he fancied himfelf
highly.

highly gratified with the companion he had selected; and he was much too warm an advocate for what he esteemed an injured character to permit the countess to continue neutral. Fitzosborne's affected dejection soon interested her feeling heart; and, though she could scarcely consider the loss of an Arabella to be a misfortune, she felt that great allowance should be made for the force of disappointment upon a mind so strongly susceptible. Still incredulous as to the reality of his attachment, she was inclined to believe, that after he had acceded to the proposals of his friends, a sense of honour and the force of habit had produced in his refined disposition a recurrence of the same images, which might be almost supposed equivalent to preference. The void which female caprice had left in his imagination must be at present painful, and though

though an enlightened understanding
would soon occupy the chasm with a
more brilliant set of ideas, delicate sensibility might be allowed to start at the
illiberal ridicule which a censorious
world is ever ready to bestow on a
jilted swain or a forsaken damsel. Beside, without being mercenary, might
not a prudent man regret the loss of a
splendid establishment? To soften that
regret she exerted all the brilliant powers
of her mind, and all the fascinating
graces of her numerous accomplish-
ments. Charmed out of his pretended
melancholy, Fitzosborne seemed to bestow a listless attention, varying the
contour of his expressions as the style of
her attractions required: Sometimes
terminating his silent adulation by ex-
claiming, "Happy Monteith!" At
another expatiating in praise of friendship; or, if he aimed at making the
                                    most

moſt forcible impreſſion, he only interrupted the vivacity of her tones by
the frequency of his ſighs.   But in either
inſtance he was equally careful that lord
Monteith ſhould hear both the exclama-
tions and the ſighs.

Diſappointed by perceiving that his
dejection did not yield to time, and
more than ever convinced that love
could not have made ſuch an incurable
wound, the counteſs began to ſuſpect
that this diſorder was conſtitutional, and
ſhe propoſed his applying to ſociety and
change of ſcene, the uſual recipe for a
melancholic humour.   His conſtant rejection of invitations induced her to
pique his pride.   " Do you know,"
ſaid ſhe, " that lady Arabella flouriſhes
" in the firſt circles, and is become ſo
" very irreſiſtible, that not only wits
" and beaus write madrigals to her, but
" a cer-

" a certain young duke of our acquaint-
" ance is thought to be ferioufly en-
" tangled ? They are to be at the opera
" together to-night in his grace's box.
" Now I intend to go, and take you for
" my *cecifbeo*. What fay you to my
" fcheme ? It will be generous to fhew
" the young adventurer how Armida
" metamorphofes her knights before he
" is irrecoverably enchanted."

" I am very willing to exhibit my
" woe-begone face, if the publication
" of it will afford you any amufement,"
returned Fitzofborne. " The duke
" and I fhall not exchange any angry
" glances, and I honour lady Arabella's
" fincerity too much to feel any refent-
" ment at her conduct. She has only
" exercifed the indubitable right of
" every human being. Her heart has
" changed its poffeffor, and fhe has
" obeyed its dictates."

" Does

" Does not your candour grant rather
" too great a latitude here?" inquired
the countefs.

" Confidering the prejudices of the
" times, I certainly do. But is there
" not a great degree of cruelty in re-
" quiring conftancy from thofe minds
" that have not fufficient fortitude to be
" really immutable? And after all, as
" we can only affume the appearance of
" it, is it not alfo unjuft, and wicked
" too, as we create a neceffity for hypo-
" crify? To difeafes in different confti-
" tutions we prefcribe different reme-
" dies; but the diforders of the mind
" muft all be cured by one univerfal
" panacea. Surely it is only the tyranny
" of cuftom that prevents us from adapt-
" ing our moral code to every chara&ter,
" inftead of ftretching diffimilar minds
" on the gigantic iron couch defigned
" for a Procruftes."

Lady

Lady Monteith felt startled. She recollected that where much was given much would be required; yet this text related to diffimilar powers of doing good, and could not poffibly be urged in extenuation of any vicious action. But Fitzofborne interrupted her mufings by affuming a gayer air than he had lately exhibited. "I fee," faid he, "I fhall have fome difficulty to "reconcile you to *all* my opinions; "but, no matter; when I legiflate for "the world, don't flatter yourfelf, that "I fhall propofe a lax fyftem to you. "I know how to eftimate your mental "ability, and *your* code fhall be rigorous "and coercive."

"Dare you repeat this fpeech to-"night at the opera in the hearing of "lady Arabella?" faid the countefs.

"There requires no courage to re-"peat an undifputed truth in the hear-

"ing

" ing of the whole world." Lady
Monteith forgot her difapprobation of
the novelty, fingularity, and laxity of
Fitzofborne's opinions; and as fhe
drove to form her party for the evening, fhe only remembered his happy
talent at a compliment.

CHAP. XXVIII.

It is Jealousy's peculiar nature
To swell small things to great; nay out of nothing
To conjure much.

YOUNG.

THE polite world were so engrossed by engagements, that lady Monteith found it impossible to form a party to her satisfaction. Exclusive of the pale votaries, who sacrifice peace, health, fortune, and honour at the shrine of Pharo, several were engaged to the Quizzes, and more to the Cabinet of Monkies, which was just opened. The fair countess could scarcely get any body into her party but those who were left out of all others: and they who refused her secretly laughed at the rusticity of supposing

poſing any body, who lived in the world, could defer till two o'clock the important buſineſs of fixing the evening occupation. She was forced to be contented with an antiquated belle of the laſt age, and a would-be fine lady of the preſent, to whom ſhe was lucky enough to add a beau, ſir Hargrave Nappy, a gentleman, who though known by every body to be incurably deaf, had long laboured under the tantalizing deſire of wiſhing to be thought a connoiſſeur in muſic. With this deſign he conſtantly attended the opera, where his unvarying countenance and fixed poſture procured him the appellation of the pillar of melody.

Surrounded by the groupe I have deſcribed, and eſcorted by the gallant Edward Fitzoſborne, lady Monteith entered a ſide-box oppoſite to that which was occupied by lady Arabella's

party. Had Geraldine intended to have
felected foils for her own perfon, the
females in her train were moft happily
gifted by nature for that purpofe; and
in point of celebrity they were juft
enough known to make it difficult for
any lady to decline being their companion. Repeated mortifications had
taught them the arcana of high life; and
the protection of a countefs was fufficiently flattering to confine them to that
humble part which they fuppofed her
ladyfhip intended they fhould fuftain.
Claiming fir Hargrave for their fhare
of the beaus, they invited him to feat
himfelf between them, and they addreffed all their obfervations to him,
without once turning their heads to
liften to the converfation which paffed
behind them. But fir Hargrave was fo
abforbed in opera ecftafies, that unlefs
his eye happened to inform him that he
was

was peculiarly addreffed, all the *fmart things* paffed utterly unnoticed.   Indeed the only honour that they ever received was a half bend, after which the amateur refumed his former erect pofition, and with one hand in his bofom, and the other (on which was a fine antique) beating time on the front of the box, he repeated, like Shakefpeare's Lorenzo, " Mark the mufic."

It is a very great pity that thefe unfortunate *fmart things* fhould be wholly loft. The prefcient Mufe at leaft muft be fuppofed to have heard them ; but I feel fo anxious to return to the reft of the party, that I muft defer the recapitulation of them to fome other opportunity, promifing, if poffible, either to interweave them with the hiftory of my travels, or, if I have no other means of introduction, to give them to the world in the form of " More laſt words of Mrs. Prudentia."

The blooming Geraldine never appeared ſo enchanting. She perceived, with a degree of pleaſure, in which ſhe did not ſuſpect any criminality, that the adventures of her box proved infinitely more intereſting to lady Arabella, than the devoirs of the noble duke whom ſhe wiſhed to exhibit as her captive. Fitz-oſborne was in excellent ſpirits. The counteſs enjoyed the circumſtance. She thought he had been extremely ill uſed, and ſhe applauded the ſpirit which could repay inſult with contempt. His attentions to herſelf, conſidered in this point of view, gave her ſincere ſatisfaction. She returned them. Her natural vivacity, combining with accidental circumſtances, hurried her into a degree of mirth, which, to thoſe who were unacquainted with its motives, appeared

peared to border upon coquetry, more
than the innocence of her heart and the
rectitude of her principles would have
permitted.

But while the lamb, basking in the
blaze of noon, bounds over the flowery
hillock, the wolf watches its haunts and
meditates its destruction. To exemplify
my pastoral simile: Fitzosborne saw with
diabolical exultation, that Geraldine's
behaviour had attracted general attention. He doubted not but calumny
would be ready to frame some malignant
whisper, and he understood the maxim
which teaches that " virtue rarely sur-
vives the loss of reputation." Though
he conceived that the powers of his own
invention were fully equal to overthrow
any defence which lady Monteith might
make, he did not disdain adventitious
aid. His watchful eye, though seem-
ingly only fixed on the lovely form

which

which was feated by him, had difcovered
lord Monteith in the pit. He perceived too that he was attentive to his
lady's behaviour, and he fancied he read
difpleafure in his countenance. " Can
" this thoughtlefs animal," faid Fitzofborne to himfelf, " have any thing
" like jealoufy in his compofition? He
" feems lefs carelefs than ufual. If fo,
" it is indeed above my hopes."

While he ruminated on this idea,
the door of the box opened, and a
young man of fafhion ftepped in. He
was an intimate friend of lord Monteith's; and, feeing the countefs in
what he thought a new point of view,
he was defirous of fharing the pleafure
which her converfation afforded. This
did not increafe the gaiety of the party.
The appearance of a ftranger caufed a
temporary interruption. Geraldine recollected her thoughts, and her natural
delicacy

delicacy fhrunk from an intrufion which, though fanctioned by the freedom of our prefent fyftem of manners, feemed inconfiftent with ftrict politenefs. His ftyle of addrefs too was bold and familiar, very different from the infinuating fenfibility of Fitzofborne, who, though confcious of diftinction, never appeared to prefume upon favour. She determined to mark her approbation of his behaviour by her own conduct, and, inftead of the confidence and vivacity which marked her deportment previous to the entrance of her new gueft, fhe became as cold and circumfcribed in her anfwers as the rules of civility could poffibly admit.

Lord Monteith now entered the box; and, as he never concealed any fentiment, the difpleafure he felt was ftrongly marked in his countenance. He had

L 4   heard

heard his lady pointed out as uncommonly beautiful by a ſtranger who ſat next him; and though he was very well pleaſed with that plaudit, the ſubſequent obſervations were not ſatisfactory. To the words, " Charming creature!" were added, " and ſo gay, ſo lively too " in her manners! what a happy man " that gentleman muſt be!" The ſtranger was juſt arrived from the country, and unwittingly ſuppoſed that a married pair would not forfeit their claims to celebrity by appearing at the ſame entertainment in the ſame party. Every exclamation which he uttered in compliment of the affection-ate attention of this peerleſs couple in-creaſed the earl's reſtleſſneſs; and, no longer able to conceal his own right to the charmer who thus faſcinated all eyes, he ſuddenly roſe and joined her. He had ſeen nothing in her manner
                                    which

which cuftom did not juftify, and Fitzofborne was of all others the friend in
whom he could moft confide. Yet,
without knowing what to blame, he
thought the laws of cuftom required
revifal.

Geraldine had not that fpecies of fortitude which fees difpleafure on a hufband's brow without any fentiment but
exultation. She was ignorant of thofe
principles which teach the diffipated
wife who has long renounced the power
of pleafing to exult in the capacity of
giving pain. The light heart which
had prompted the gay repartee became
loaded with fudden depreffion, and the
frolic fmile vanifhed with the unaffected
vivacity which had given it birth.

The world had much to fay on the
adventures of this evening. Poor Arabella! every body was very forry for
her. Lady Monteith had certainly

L 5 fpirited

spirited away her lover. Her exultation upon the occasion was rather too marked for a woman of prodigious decorum; and really, if she did continue to flirt it so notoriously in public, she must renounce her pretensions to such *very* strict propriety, and consent to be thought no better than other people.

At coming out of the opera Fitzofborne tapped lord Monteith upon the shoulder, and asked him, how he disposed of himself for the evening. " At home, if you have nothing better to " propose:" was the answer. " There is " a spirited set just gone to Brookes's," continued Fitzofborne; " suppose we " follow them to observe manners and " characters." His lordship had no objection.

Early in lord Monteith's life his name was unfortunately familiar to the
frequenters

frequenters of the gaming-table and the heroes of the turf. His attachment to the lovely Geraldine leffened that dangerous propenfity; and, though fhe had failed in her endeavours to infpire a love of elegant pleafures, indifference for his former purfuits had gradually increafed to difguft: the lefs pernicious fports of the field, and a boyifh turn of amufement, fucceeding in occupying a mind too volatile to feek pleafure out of its own refources. But fince his lordfhip's difguft and forbearance arofe more from the abfence of temptation than from any fixed principle, the fight of the card table and the rattle of the dice-box excited paffions which increafed the unfubdued emotion that he had felt at the opera.

He propofed to Fitzofborne to form a party. Edward pleaded a total want of fkill; protefted, that he had a fixed abhor-

L. 6.

abhorrence of the gaming-table; and declared, that he never visited those scenes, except to study the human character, and to moralize on the fatal effects of the impetuous passion of avarice. His reflections were soon finished that evening, for in a little time he professed himself wearied with the scene, and he proposed to lord Monteith that they should retire to a private room. There too he felt the moments drag heavily, and it was mutually agreed to enliven them by a friendly game at picquet.

The stake first proposed was trifling: Monteith was unsuccessful. He transferred his latent resentment to the cards, which he stamped under his foot; called for a new pack, and insisted upon doubling the sum they played for. The events of the evening put several hundreds into Fitzosborne's pocket; and his success might still have been greater, but

but neither his friendſhip nor his honour would (he proteſted) permit him to urge his good fortune any further. "Your temper," ſaid he, "is too "warm ; and I hope the little vexations "of this evening will convince you of "the neceſſity of ſelf-control, or at leaſt "prevent you from trying your chance "with thoſe who might take the un- "generous advantage of your agitation, "which I ſcorn to uſe."

"I value not money," ſaid Monteith angrily ! "nor can the curſed cards agi- "tate me. A truce with your morality "therefore, Edward ; when I want a "monitor, it is time enough for you to "inveſt yourſelf with that dignity."

"I am not in a reſentful humour," returned Fitzoſborne ſmiling. "I ſhall "therefore very gladly reſign my dig- "nity, as you term it. Indeed, I have "been a little unlucky in the exerciſe
7   "of

"of it this evening. Yet if my well-
"meant admonitions are but remem-
"bered by my friends, the difintereft-
"ednefs of my attachment will enable
"me to fupport a little tranfient acri-
"mony."

"Where elfe did you play the lec-
"turer?" inquired Monteith, carelefsly.

"Where I faw a little impropriety,"
replied Fitzofborne, with fuppreffed fig-
nificance.

"And did you fucceed no better
"than you have done with me?" continued the earl, with increafing anxiety.

"I don't know. The character I
"had to deal with was more *guarded*
"than you are."

"What caufed your reproof?" faid
his lordfhip, with affected eafe, and apparently occupied in forting the cards
into three divifions.

"I be--

" I believe nothing but the too great
" nicety of my own feelings : for on re-
" viewing the affair I cannot fee any
" thing effentially wrong ; and I begin
" to think thofe rules which impofe
" fuperior caution on perfons who are
" objects of public admiration unnecef-
" farily fevere."

" The fentiments of ladies," refumed
Monteith, " are generally more delicate
" in thefe points than thofe of men:
" Suppofe you make Geraldine your
" cafuift in this bufinefs ? She will tell
" you if you went too far in your ad-
" monitions."

" By no means," faid Fitzofborne,
fnatching the cards. " Come, enough
" of one fubject. Shall we have an-
" other game ?"

" No! I am tired ; and as I love to
" have every doubtful bufinefs cleared
" up, we will go home to fupper, and
" I will

" I will mention your uneafinefs to lady
" Monteith, that you may fleep with a
" difburdened confcience."

Fitzofborne ftarted. " How came
" *you* to difcover that the hafty opi-
" nion which I injudicioufly uttered,
" really difpleafed her? Let me con-
" jure you, my lord, by all our friend-
" fhip, endeavour to reftore me to her
" favour, and be convinced that I can
" only have forfeited it through inad-
" vertence."

Lord Monteith fmiled with the confcious fuperiority which attends a fuccefsful feint, and affured the alarmed
Fitzofborne, that, if he would candidly
acknowledge the nature of his offence,
he might depend upon his interpofition.

" It really," returned Edward, " was
" nothing of confequence. You have
" often charged me with poffeffing a
" ftoical fternnefs, and I confefs fome
                                    " of

" of my notions are auftere. The
" countefs was in very lively fpirits
" this evening."

" Was fhe ?" faid Monteith, biting
his lips.

" I faid fomething to her, I forget
" what, refpecting the eafe with which
" Britifh matrons publicly permit the
" advances of notorious libertines. I
" beg your pardon, Monteith, I know
" he is your friend; but I muft own I
" repeated this with more energy when
" fir Richard Vernon came into the
" box. You know his notions are
" avowedly licentious."

" It was very friendly of you," exclaimed his lordfhip, with a voice con-
vulfed with paffion. " Did he talk to
" lady Monteith in an improper ftyle ?"

" By no means. Yet there was fome-
" what freer in his addrefs than I fhould
" have approved had the lady been my
                              " wife ;

" wife; and I felt for my abfent friend.
" The blaze of your Geraldine's charms,
" my lord, is loft upon me.   Beauty can
" never more affect my heart.   But
" I too well recollect the emotions it
" has caufed not to wifh fir Richard to
" avoid lady Monteith, at leaft if he
" refpects his own tranquillity."

" And could Geraldine refent your
" friendly obfervation?" interrupted
Monteith.

" She only anfwered, that I was grown
" fplenetic, for public places fanctioned
" thefe intrufions.   I however obferved,
" that fhe did not fpeak to me any more
" during the whole evening."

" I deteft caprice.   She fhall ac-
" knowledge the friendlinefs of your
" motives."

" Oh! for heaven's fake! do not in-
" terfere in that ftyle.   You will alarm
" her pride, and fink me for ever in her
                                    " opinion.

" opinion. Befide, you will utterly pre-
" vent any future effort on my part
" gently to reftrain thofe very agreeable
" fpirits which may be liable to mifcon-
" ftruction. To own the truth, I thought
" to-night fhe attracted particular atten-
" tion."

" Her prudence," exclaimed the earl,
who, though he had imbibed the poifon
of infinuation, was yet offended by a
direct attack, " is as exemplary as her
" character is fpotlefs."

" True," replied Fitzofborne ; " but
" think of the malignity of the
" world."

" Who dares to impeach her con-
" duct ?" continued her lord, with increafed violence.

" What does not envy and calumny
" dare ?" cried the fentimental torturer.
" But I fee my friendfhip is troublefome.
" However, Monteith, recollect, that
" you

" you artfully wound the fecret out of
" me, and therefore have no right to be
" difpleafed at the difclofure."

" Your hand, Edward. Excufe my
" warmth. My wife is too dear to me,
" to allow me to hear the leaft cenfure
" caft upon her behaviour with indif-
" ference. I venerate the excellence of
" your heart, and I love your franknefs.
" I am frank myfelf, though I own I
" did ufe a little circumlocution to dif-
" cover what you certainly never in-
" tended me to know. I was too fubtle
" there. Was I not ? But come, think
" no more of it. Perhaps lady Mon-
" teith might be a little wrong; but I
" know you both meant well, and fhe
" will readily forgive you."

" Then, as a pledge of your renewed
" efteem, let me entreat you never to
" mention this affair to her. I may
" have been too fufceptible, and have
                              " miftaken

" miſtaken her ſilence for reſentment ;
" for I am convinced I miſconſtrued
" her preceding behaviour."

Monteith pledged his honour for
ſecreſy, and endeavoured to diſſipate his
chagrin by humming an air. But the
idea that Fitzoſborne had ſeen ſome-
thing wrong in Geraldine, and his recollection of the ſtranger's converſation,
ſunk deep into his mind, and clouded
the gay vacuity of his thoughts with
ſpectres fearful as " the green-eyed
monſter" which haunted the frank and
noble Moor, who, like lord Monteith,
" thought men honeſt who but ſeemed
to be ſo."

CHAP. XXIX.

No might nor greatnefs in mortality
Can Cenfure 'fcape ; back-wounding Calumny
The whiteft virtue ftrikes.

SHAKESPEARE.

VICE always appears to be moft alluring when its machinations are crowned with fuccefs. During the dangerous period of youth, while the paffions are warm, the imagination lively, and the judgment weak, the fpectator feels a bias in favour of that adventurer whofe courfe (marked by ingenuity) leads to a fpeedy attainment of his defires. But could Inexperience reflect, and Impetuofity paufe, the couch of even the moft profperous villain would prefent no alluring fpectacle. Fitzofborne's plans had hitherto anfwered his wifhes. His fpecious

manners

manners had acquired the esteem of the
countess, and the unbounded confidence
of her lord.   He had obtained a firm
footing in the family; had sown the
baleful germ of suspicion, so fatal to domestic peace; and the displeasure and
gloom which occasionally pervaded lord
Monteith's countenance convinced him
that it had taken root.   Calumny was
prepared to doubt the stability of Geraldine's honour; and Calumny, like a
pestilential blast, can taint the innocence
it assails.   To these engines of seduction
might be added the sophistical principles
of false philosophy, which, though
cautiously administered and often reject-
ed, still, like the delved mine, possess a
power capable of subverting the firmest
moral virtue, if not founded on the rock
of religion.

Yet Fitzosborne was wretched.   The
atrocity of his designs haunted his pillow,

not

not with a fenfe of remorfe, but with the
apprehenfion of danger. The fituation
of the lady was exalted; her charaćter
was exemplary; her connećtions were
refpećtable; her hufband, as he had
lately difcovered, was not only tenacious
of her reputation, and vain of her at-
trаćtions, but alfo confcious of her
merits, and fincérely attached to her
perfon. Though the earl's apprehenfion
was peculiarly flow, his paffions were as
remarkably vehement; and his fkill at
the various offenfive weapons was fo
great, that his opponent could have
very little chance of efcaping with life,
if called to make the *amende honorable*.
Fitzofborne's fortunes were almoft de-
fperate. Worldly prudence feemed,
therefore, to point out the neceffity of
applying his ingenuity in devifing fome
plan of improving his circumftances,
inftead of wafting his talents in a purfuit
which

which only promifed danger, or, to fpeak according to his ideas, " barren honour."

Notwithftanding the appearance of open hoftility, he held a private corre- fpondence with the vifcount's family; and his intelligence from thence con- firmed his own opinion, that the breach with lady Arabella was not totally irre- parable. Her vexation at his attention to lady Monteith was too lively to be concealed, and too fincere to yield to the hopes which the noble duke's in- creafing admiration infpired. In vain did fhe recollect detecting him incognito at the theatre, looking at her through his opera-glafs. In vain did fhe re- member her more fplendid triumph, when he prefented her with a ticket for lady Fillagree's fancied ball, infcribed " To the faireft." Fitzofborne faw his affiduities without emotion. The noble

duke's sentiments were known to be in-
auspicious to marriage; and no lady,
who had not absolutely determined to
be a duchess, could even affect to find
satisfaction in his conversation.

Fitzosborne poized the chance of lucrative advantage with precision; and,
as he had no inclination for sleeping in
the bed of honour, he bestowed some
forethought on the hazards he ran by
pursuing his illicit designs against the
lovely countess. Since he deemed his
success certain, it was unnecessary to
examine the effect of a disappointment.
Great prudence, great caution, and great
morality, might prevent a *rencontre*.
He might be unwilling to lift his arm
against the life of his friend; he might
respect the laws of his country; or his
health might impose the necessity of a
tour for its restoration. The last step
would be the most convenient, in case
lord

lord Monteith applied for legal damages, since, however large the fum given by the verdict, abfence and incapacity would be a receipt in full. The next ftep of the injured hufband muft be a divorce, and the deferted lady could not then object to taking refuge in a fecond marriage, which was the only chance of reftoring her again to the world, if not with untainted, at leaft with a convalefcent character. Geraldine was an heirefs, and it was to be fuppofed that her fettlements were made with proper precaution. Even as a wife fhe was infinitely more defirable than Arabella; and, though the illiberality of hufbands might wifh to fecure their domeftic poffeffions by an impaffable inclofure, modern fpirit had proved itfelf able to furmount every fence; and the lady might give away herfelf and her property feveral times over, without calling upon

M 2   death

death to cancel a former bond. The world indeed would at firſt be angry; but the times were very liberal. People would allow for the force of *irreſiſtible* temptation. They would plead, that it was impoſſible to forbear adoring ſuch a charming creature. The blame would be happily transferred to my lord, who ought never to have admitted a friend into his family, or to have truſted her out of his ſight; and in a little time every body would viſit Mr. Fitzoſborne and his lady, and perhaps even find them out to be a very worthy and exemplary pair.

Confirmed in his deſigns not more by his own inſidious inclinations than by the falſe notions which prevail even amongſt the more principled part of that important circle called the great world, Fitzoſborne proſecuted his nefarious plans; and he determined, that if

fear,

fear, or as he called it prudence, did not check, compunction should not dissuade. Chance, and the credulous confidence of lord Monteith, favoured his wishes. Cards of invitation to lady Fillagree's *petit soupé* had been sent to the Monteiths, and the countess had not only chosen her character, but she had also decorated an Italian tiffany with festoons of violets, in which dress she intended to personify the Perdita of Shakespeare. Her anxious entreaties had prevailed upon her lord to accompany her in the habit of the royal Florizel; and this mark of attachment on her part, and condescension on his, promised the renewal of domestic harmony. The expected evening approached, when a note from the minister requested lord Monteith's attendance in the house of peers. Business of great importance was to be agitated;

a vio-

a violent oppofition was expected; and
the honour of his lordfhip's fupport
would confer a lafting obligation. The
earl was not in the habit of courting
minifterial favour; he difliked the tafk
of attendance; and the labour of liftening to a long debate was always fufficiently terrific to make him prejudge
the queftion. Yet though no one ever
took lefs pains to acquire real authority,
he was very well pleafed to be thought
a man of confequence; and the minifter's
requeft was too preffing to be declined.
Geraldine wifhed to give up her engagement; but my lord had fixed upon
a plan that would fettle every thing,
and to which his own diflike of mafked
balls and fancy fuppers gave a determi-
nate ftability. It was, that Fitzofborne,
inftead of fpending the evening alone in
the library, fhould be her efcort. My
lord's drefs would fit him pretty exactly,
                                    and

and Edward's excufes anfwered the end
for which they were defigned, which
was to fix my lord moft pofitively in
his determinations.

The entertainment was to be given
at a villa a little diftance from town.
Geraldine dreffed early; but her heavy
heart feemed to anticipate fome difaftrous
iffue. My lord came into her dreffing-
room to fee if fhe looked her character;
and while he contemplated the fimplicity
and exquifite adaption of her ornaments,
the apprehenfions with which he had
been lately tortured returned. "Do
" not," faid he, " dance with Vernon;
" nor any of that fet, if they fhould afk
" you. Plead that you are engaged to
" Fitzofborne, or elfe fay that you are
" tired."

"Will not that have a " fingular
" appearance?" inquired the countefs.
M 4 " You

" You have a ſtrange apprehenſive-
" neſs of ſingularity, Geraldine. Don't
" you remember your father's words,
" that there is no ſhame in being the
" only perſon who acts as ſhe ought
" to do ?"

" Suppoſe then," ſaid her ladyſhip,
" I do not dance at all."

" What ! when all the world knows
" that you are very fond of dancing ?
" Is that the way to avoid ſingularity ?
" And why this averſion to my friend ?
" Cannot you forgive him for offering
" you ſome advice which you was too
" careleſs to attend to ?"

" My dear lord, there has been ſome
" little miſunderſtanding, certainly. I
" am far from having any averſion to
" Fitzoſborne, and as far from being
" offended at his giving me any advice. I
" do not even recollect the circumſtance."

" O ! you

" O! you give it that turn, do you?
" But you underſtand my preſent pro-
" hibition, I ſuppoſe, and you will re-
" member it."

" Undoubtedly. And do you re-
" collect, that depending upon your
" accompanying me, I have not formed
" any party. If poſſible come away
" from the houſe, and join me at
" Richmond."

" You are grown a coward, Geral-
" dine. However I will come, if I can;
" but Fitzoſborne is ſurely a ſufficient
" guard. Tell Arabella to do that worthy
" fellow juſtice, or I ſhall diſown her for
" my ſiſter."

The vivacity of lady Monteith had
received ſo ſevere a check that ſhe
could not recover her ſpirits during
her ride to lady Fillagree's. Fitzoſborne
diſcovered her dejection. " I know,"
ſaid he, " ſuch ſolicitude is often very

M 5   " trouble-

" troublesome ; yet the fervency of my
" friendship will not permit me to see
" you difpirited without inquiring into
" the caufe of your depreffion."

" It is fo wholly feminine," returned
fhe, " that it is abfolutely undefinable,
" and muft be fet down in the catalogue
" of my unaccountables, unlefs I fhould
" give as a reafon, what I am very un-
" willing to admit ; I mean, an idea of
" my lord's, that fome time or another
" I did not treat your good advice with
" fufficient deference. Pray, Fitzofborne,
" when did you play the moralift ; and
" when was I fuch a refractory pupil ?"

" Ah Monteith ! this is one of thy
" mifconceptions. I will explain the
" whole affair, madam, though it is too
" ridiculous to merit repetition. You
" recollect the night we were together
" at the opera."

" Perfectly."

" And

" And that in return to some observa-
" tions which I made on the behaviour
" of lady Arabella, you said, disappoint-
" ment had made me splenetic?"

" I do."

" Lord Monteith heard your answer
" as he entered the box; and he will
" persist in his opinion, that my ex-
" pressions were pointed at you, as a
" reproof for something in your manner
" to Vernon. I must excuse him by
" saying, that he was a little flustered.
" I followed him to Brookes's, where
" we soon adjusted ——"

" To Brookes's! Does my lord fre-
" quent Brookes's?"

" O you tempter! No; I have too
" much honour to reveal secrets. The
" affair was soon explained, I was going
" to say;—for Monteith really has a very
" good heart, which excuses a little
" accidental puzzle-patedness."

Geraldine coloured; but her Proteus companion gave her no time to resent. Looking out of the chariot window, he relapsed into sentiment. "See, dear "lady Monteith," said he, "how the "giddy throng hasten to this festival of "ostentatious vanity. A reflecting "mind, on contemplating this crowd of "carriages, must feel other sensations "than those of pleasure. Not to men-"tion the sufferings of those noble ani-"mals who draw the vehicles of tyrant "man, the situation of master and ser-"vant, as exhibited upon the present "occasion, is enough to cure the most "obdurate heart of its partiality for "those distinctions of rank which cor-"rupt society now exhibits. How re-"pugnant to the feelings of universal "love is that pale emaciated footman, "who, exposed to the inclemency of "the seasons, suspends the flambeau

5 "over

" over the carriage of his voluptuous
" mafter! How remote muft that man
" ftill be from the ultimate perfection of
" his nature, who can enjoy the pleafures
" of a crowded affembly, while his
" coachman quakes in the warping
" wind, or fhrinks beneath the pelting
" ftorm! It is the cruelty of a Mezen-
" tius: The living body is united to
" putridity."

" There is fome juftice in your obfervations," faid the countefs: " and
" it behoves us as *individuals* to leffen
" the evils of that inequality which
" public good requires." The carriages
now ftopped; and as Fitzofborne led
her to the gay affemblage of beauty,
fancy, and elegance, her reflections on
his character concluded with an obfervation, that " his very failings leaned to
the fide of virtue."

The

The ball went on very much like other balls. Sir Richard Vernon and several gentlemen of his caſt of character were preſent, and Geraldine complied punctually with her lord's injunction, either to ſit down, or to dance with Fitzoſborne. She had forgot to account for his appearing in a dreſs ſo correſpondent to her own; and when ſome ladies, by pointing it out, alarmed her ſenſe of propriety, her explanation was embarraſſed, and conſequently ſuſpicious. As at the opera, Fitzoſborne's attentions were confined to her; and his elegant addreſs and polite vivacity added the ſneer of envy to the whiſper of detraction. Lady Arabella had indeed the honour to move down one dance with the duke; but his grace was ſo fatigued by the exertion, that he was obliged to renounce dancing, and to

have

have recourse to Caflino for the reft of
the evening. Her fucceeding partners
ranked no higher than commoners,
without poffeffing any of the innate dif-
tinctions which gave celebrity to the
partner of Fitzofborne. He had only
bowed to her in the moft diftant manner poffible. Her fmile of invitation
was unanfwered; and fhe began to
think a fainting fit was the only chance
of roufing the monfter's attention. She
performed it in the greateft perfection;
but on opening her eyes fhe felt a little
mortified to find, that neither he nor
the countefs appeared in the circle
which had gathered round her. Another
glance convinced her, that they were
not in the room.

"The heat of this apartment," faid
the lovely fufferer, "is infupportable.
"Do, my deareft Harriet, lend me
"your arm, and let me breathe a little
"pure

" pure air in the veſtibule." The viſcounteſs complied, and the miſtreſs of
the ceremony with ſeveral other ladies
accompanied the fair invalid.

Lady Arabella caſt a ſcrutinizing
glance upon the ſuite of chambers
through which ſhe was led; but ſhe
deſcended into the veſtibule without
making any diſcovery. It had been
converted into an orangery for the occaſion, and decorated with a variety of
lamps taſtefully ſuſpended. The many-
coloured light trembling on the fragrant
exotics, the freſhneſs of the air, the ſtill-
neſs of the ſcene, and the extenſive view
which it admitted of the " ſtars in all
their ſplendor" and " the moon walking
in brightneſs," afforded a ſtriking
contraſt to the glittering but artificial
ſcene which they had juſt left. Lady
Arabella and her friends were not the
only admirers of its enchanting effect,

for

for at the upper end stood the countess and Fitzosborne.

"Pray let us go back," shrieked lady Arabella, who however did not much doubt their identity. "I am "quite frightened. Somebody is here." The lady of the house declared, that it could be nobody whom she could object to, while the charitable viscountess whispered, "that it would be rude to "interrupt a private party."

"Oh! not for the universe," exclaimed Arabella. "I would die a thousand "deaths rather than be rude."

The countess advanced with an air of easy dignity, which the inquisitive looks of the other ladies soon discomposed. "Bless me, sister," said the candid Arabella, "I really did not think it was "you."—"And Edward too," continued the significant lady Fitzosborne; "how "do you do? There is no such thing

"as

" as catching your attention for one
" moment this evening. How came
" your aufterity to condefcend to vifit
" thefe tinfel amufements?"

" Pardon me, madam," faid Edward,
bowing refpectfully to lady Arabella,
" thofe amufements cannot be tinfel
" which have the power of attracting
" fterling merit." Her ladyfhip did
not deign to take the leaft notice of
his fubmiffion, but continued whifpering
the countefs: " So you have one con-
" ftant *cecifbeo* I fee, and Monteith ftays
" at home. Very fingular, I vow. But
" was you not afraid of taking cold
" during this long converfation?"

" No," replied Geraldine with recovered compofure; " our converfa-
" tion was too interefting for me to
" think of cold. What if I fhould tell
" you, Arabella, that fome part of it
" related to yourfelf. But you really
" treat

" treat your faithful fwain's advances in
" too contemptuous a ftyle for me to
" begin my requefted interceffion, or
" even to deliver to you a meffage
" from your brother on the fame fub-
" ject."

The party had now re-entered the
houfe, when the countefs, turning, faid
to Fitzofborne, " You forget Mifs Par-
" ker."—" Where is Mifs Parker?"
was the general inquiry. " In the
" orangery," faid lady Monteith. " No,
" madam, I am here," echoed a fhrill
voice, which iffued from one of the
ladies who accompanied lady Arabella.

" Mifs Parker could not have been
" left in the orangery," obferved the
vifcountefs. " Your ladyfhip was cer-
" tainly miftaken. She came down
" ftairs with us,"

" And

" And she was the first who support-
" ed me when I fainted," said lady Arabella, who, in her eagerness to detect a
supposed criminal, forgot, that fainting
people do not always know what passes.

" She certainly accompanied me into
" the orangery," repeated lady Monteith.

Miss Parker, who was no other than
the " antiquated belle" at the opera,
now came forward, and with a respect-
ful courtesy, begged leave to explain:
" I certainly accompanied your lady-
" ship and Mr. Fitzosborne down stairs,
" when you did me the honour to ask
" me ; but while your ladyship was en-
" gaged with him in looking at the
" stars, I found it was very cold, and I
" was afraid of my old attack in my
" shoulder; so I thought I would step
" and fetch my pellice ; and I believe
                                    " your

" your ladyſhip and the gentleman were
" too much occupied to perceive that I
" was gone."

A ſarcaſtic ſmile, which lady Fillagree's politeneſs could ſcarcely reſtrain
her from joining, followed this narrative, when Edward, like Joſeph Sur-
face, promiſed to give a full and ſatisfactory account of the matter.   He
ſaid, that on his mentioning that he
had obſerved a beautiful Jacobea lily
in full blow as they entered, lady
Monteith and Miſs Parker had expreſſed a wiſh to pay it more attention; that he had the honour to
eſcort them; and that, after admiring
the flower, her ladyſhip was ſuddenly
ſtruck by the ſplendor of ſome particular conſtellations, when lady Arabella
entered.

Another general ſmile enſued, and
Geraldine, no longer able to rally her
                                   ſpirits,

fpirits, ordered her chariot; and, telling
Mifs Parker fhe would fet her down at
her own door, fhe relieved the ladies
from the pain of fuppreffed merriment,
by taking leave.

CHAP. XXX.

Confcience, what art thou? Thou tremendous power!
Who doft inhabit us without our leave;—
How doft thou light a torch to diftant deeds!
Make the paft, prefent, and the future, frown!
How, ever and anon, awake the foul,
As with a peal of thunder!

YOUNG.

THE fuppofed fecret, mentioned in my laft Chapter, was of too much importance to be confined to the difcoverers. By means of the happy art of inuendoes, the initiated foon diffeminated it through the whole circle, in the politeft manner imaginable. One lady obferved, that the adventures of the third Eloifa would foon be publifhed: another affirmed, that it would be called Werter the Second, with a different cataftrophe: a third wifhed to read the Chapter on Botany:

a fourth

a fourth thought that that on aftronomy
would contain the moft aftonifhing dif-
covery: a fifth allowed, that aftronomy
and botany were both very fuitable
ftudies for fhepherds and fhepherdeffes;
and every body hoped that the adventures of the poor little lady, who had
loft her pellice, and got the rheumatifm,
would be inferted. The farcafms of
the vifcountefs were peculiarly piquant:
for hers was the moft fufpected character in company; and it is an in-
variable rule with ladies of her caft, that
the odium with which you befpatter a
neighbour's reputation has the effect, by
retroaction, of furbifhing your own: Her
indignation was chiefly pointed at lord
Monteith, who, fhe faid, was certainly
anxious to obtain the honour of being a
cornuto; and her idea was thought to
be the more judicious, as it was known
to correfpond with the fentiments of the
noble

noble vifcount her hufband. Envy, idlenefs, the love of faying good things, and a dearth of converfation, affifted her to propagate the ftory. For two days the town talked of nothing elfe, and every relater could add circumftances of frefh atrocity. In two days more, the truth of thefe adventitious circumftances became doubtful, and, being proved unfounded, the whole fabric fell with them to the ground. At the end of the week every body was heartily forry for the dear mifreprefented countefs; and every body, forgetting the part they had themfelves taken, heartily wifhed that fome law might be invented to prevent defamation.—But to return to the object of thefe inquifitorial proceedings.

The lovely Geraldine plainly perceived the malicious explanation that had been given to an incident which

Fitzofborne had faithfully explained. The love of diftinction was, as I have before obferved, one of her ruling foibles; but fhe fought to gratify it by the nobleft means. Her fpotlefs fame added luftre to the fplendor of her talents and the attractions of her beauty. She had ever been named as one of thofe few, who, in a degenerate age, afforded a happy inftance of the poffible union of propriety and fafhion. To have the goodly edifice which fhe had reared with fuch affiduous care at once deftroyed; to have her unfullied name become the jeft of witlings and the affociate of wilful depravity, was infupportable. Even fuppofing that the candid hearer would reject the calumnious affertion, fhe could not endure the very idea of having her character expofed to fufpicious difcuffion. She fat filent in the chariot, the tear of anguifh ftealing down her cheek,

incapable

incapable of attending to Miſs Parker's narrative, whoſe regret about the pellice furniſhed her with a ſubject of lamentation till they arrived in town.

Fitzoſborne read lady Monteith's ſentiments. He rightly judged that this keen ſenſibility would prove injurious to his audacious deſigns; and he determined to exert his inſidious arts to ſubdue it. The earl was not returned from the Houſe. The counteſs wiſhed him good night, and paſſed on to her dreſſing-room. Fitzoſborne followed her to the door. " Excuſe my " anxiety," ſaid he; " your look does " not indicate a wiſh for repoſe. Will " you allow me to ſit with you till " Monteith returns?" She replied, that ſhe was not in ſpirits for company; and after a pauſe, " It is in vain," ſaid ſhe, " to diſguiſe my feelings, Fitz-

" oſborne;

" ofborne ; and you know the caufe of
" my diftrefs."

" I know nothing that can juftify, or
" at leaft deferve, thofe tears. Deareft
" lady Monteith, for Heaven's fake,
" conquer that emotion, which increafes
" the mifanthropy I long have felt at
" the narrow prejudice and illiberality
" of the world."

" You are always tilting againft thofe
" windmill giants," returned Geraldine
with a languid fmile. " It is of the
" fpirit of detraction and inconfiderate-
" nefs that I complain ; of that cruel
" levity, which fports with what is
" dearer than life."

" Nay, now you urge your fenfibility
" too far. It is weaknefs, not delicacy,
" to put our happinefs fo much in the
" power of others. Have you forgot-
" ten that beautiful fentiment, ' The
" con-

" confcious mind is its own awful
" world ?'

" I grant its propriety only with re-
" fpect to the tortures of guilt; for can
" innocence be infenfible of the value
" of reputation ?"

" It may difprove flander by defpif-
" ing it, and by acting with marked
" contempt of its petty machinations.
" The tale you feem to apprehend is
" too poor, too contemptible for be-
" lief. I have but one fear refpecting
" its public expofure."

" What fear ?"

" If lord Monteith fhould hear it."

" If he fhould, what have I to
" dread ?"

" The warmth of his character;
" his irritable impetuofity; his fuf-
" picious ———"

" Sufpicious, did you fay? How
" muft I be degraded, Mr. Fitzofborne,

" in

" in his opinion! To fufpect me after
" four years experienced confidence!
" And what muft the world think of
" me, if even my firft, my deareft
" friend doubts my rectitude?"

" I know that angels are not purer;
" and when Monteith recollects himfelf,
" his judgment will tell him the fame.
" He is now a little warped; an un-
" happy ill-grounded apprehenfion—a
" fmothered fpark nearly extinguifhed
" by reafon, which this ridiculous ftory
" may revive;—and fufpicion in a cha-
" racter like his muft be terrible."

Geraldine leaned almoft fainting
againft the wainfcot. A deadly palenefs was diffufed over her intelligent
face, and her heart panted with apprehenfive terror. None, except a Domi-
tian or a Fitzofborne, who delight
in torture, but muft have pitied her
agonies.

The

The traitor did indeed affect to pity. He dropped upon his knee, and uttered every rhapsodical expression which the most guileful art could dictate. "Dearest "lady Monteith, for Heaven's sake be "composed—my tortured heart bleeds "to see your anguish—most injured— "most lovely sufferer—Oh richly wor- "thy of a better fate—Impart your "anguish to the faithful friend who "would die to relieve it."

The last words recalled her recol- lection. "Rise, sir," said she with becoming dignity. "My situation does "not call for the active offices of friend- "ship. You say I am injured. In what? "From what motive do you torture me "with suspense? You seem to possess "some fatal secret respecting me. If I "ought to know the evil you allude to, "tell me at once, that I may arm my "soul with fortitude to sustain my trials,

N 4 "or

" or detect the calumny which sports
" with my peace."

Edward was disconcerted. He had
hoped that so much friendship might
have surprized her into a little acknowledgment. And he perceived with regret that many a summer's sun must
still rise to mature his villany. He had
never yet encountered the resistance of
a firm superior mind, or so strongly
seen the " loveliness of virtue in her
own form," or " felt how awful goodness is." Yet, more remorseless than
the Prince of Darkness, " he pined not
at his own loss."

The sophists, who in these evil days
are falsely called enlightened, affect not
to palliate their own vices by pleas of
necessity and frailty, whatever disguise
they may assume to expedite their success with others. Aspiring to a pre-
eminence in impiety, which former
times

times feared to arrogate, they fin upon
principle, promulgate fyftems to juftify
iniquity, and profcribe repentance by a
morality which overturns every reftraint, and a religion that prohibits
nothing but devotion. Combining Pa-
gan fuperftitions with the exploded re-
veries of irrational theorifts, they place
at the head of their world of chance a
fupine material God, whom they recog-
nize by the name of Nature; and pretend that its worfhip fuperfedes all other
laws human and divine. By the fide
of this circumfcribed Deity they erect
the idol fhrine of its vicegerent, Intereft; by the monftrous doctrines, that
" whatever is profitable is right," that
" the end fanctifies the means," and
that " human actions ought to be free,"
they diffolve the bonds of fociety; and,
after conducting their bewildered fol-
lowers through the mazes of folly and

N 5   " guilt,

guilt, in search of an unattainable perfection, their views terminate at last in
that fallacious opiate which infidelity
presents, " the eternal sleep of death."

When posterity shall know that these
principles characterize the close of the
eighteenth century, it will cease to wonder at the calamities which history will
then have recorded. Such engines are
sufficiently powerful to overturn govern-
ments, and to shake the deep-founded
base of the firmest empires. Should it
therefore be told to future ages, that
the capricious dissolubility (if not the
absolute nullity) of the nuptial tie and
the annihilation of parental authority are
among the blasphemies uttered by the
moral instructors of these times: should
they hear, that law was branded as a
vain and even unjust attempt to bring
individual actions under the restrictions
of general rule; that chastity was de-
fined

fined to mean only individuality of affection; that religion was degraded into a sentimental effusion; and that these doctrines do not proceed from the pen of *avowed* profligates, but from persons *apparently* actuated by the desire of improving the happiness of the world: should, I say, generations yet unborn hear this, they will not ascribe the annihilation of thrones and altars to the successful arms of France, but to those principles which, by dissolving domestic confidence and undermining private worth, paved the way for universal confusion.

Stimulated by that zeal for making proselytes which marks the missionaries of these doctrines, Fitzosborne had hoped to goad his victim into the snares of infidelity by the corroding pangs of previous guilt. Her unaffected agony at the idea of her husband's doubting the propriety of her conduct

N.6   and

and the rectitude of her heart, could
only be infpired by connubial tendernefs and real delicacy. The blufh of
generous indignation which kindled
upon her cheek at the fuppofition that
Edward's infinuations might proceed
from finifter views, and the calm contempt with which fhe treated the little
arts of feduction to which female vanity has fometimes yielded, convinced
him that all his attempts to overturn
her high-feated honour would be ineffectual, unlefs he could weaken the
bonds of conjugal attachment, or remove the ftrong bulwark of confcious
immortality, which gave energy to her
principles and ftability to her virtue.
Her native fagacity affured him, that
all thefe attempts muft be made with
caution; but his poifonous noftrums,
once introduced, would work with filent
vigour. If the conflict of the paffions
fhould not be fufficiently ftormy in her
                                    tem-

temperate mind to erafe the belief of future retribution, her thirft after knowledge might entangle her in metaphyfical fubtilties. The love of diftinction and the allurements of example might induce her to add one more to thofe courageous females who conceive that the character of a woman is not entirely divefted of weaknefs till fhe defies Omnipotence; while unrequited tendernefs and unrewarded defert muft eftrange an exquifitely fufceptible heart from its unworthy mafter, and direct its affections to the fpecious blandifhments of an unprincipled impofture.

Fitzofborne's anfwer to Geraldine's fpirited appeal was dictated by the moft confummate art. He protefted that he had no fecret to divulge but what fhe already knew; namely, that lord Monteith had unwarily imbibed fome fufpicious apprehenfions from the marked admi-

admiration which fir Richard Vernon
had paid to her at the opera, and to
which the incidental circumſtance of
her being in remarkably good ſpirits
that evening might contribute. He
ſcarcely wondered at his friend's alarm,
when he conſidered the free notions of
the age, the baronet's libertine principles,
the impetuoſity of lord Monteith's temper, and his extreme ſuſceptibility in a
point of honour, which in his opinion
probably proceeded from the warmth
of his conjugal attachment. He begged
pardon for too deeply ſympathizing in
her uneaſineſs, but owned that his feelings were never proof againſt the magic
influence of female tears. The term
" injured," which he perceived had
alarmed her, was heedleſsly uttered,
without any reference, at leaſt any deſigned one, unleſs it alluded to thoſe
illiberal ſlanderers who attempted to
                              aſperſe

asperse a character which he verily believed was the only exception to that
general carelessness of reputation too
strongly characteristic of the manners of
the present race of married ladies.

" Calumny, my dear lady Monteith,"
continued he, " is now considered as
" the test of fashion ; and, instead of
" shrinking from its pestilential attack,
" even women of virtue conceive a slan-
" derous paragraph in a morning paper
" to be a kind of passport to celebrity ;
" and, pleased with becoming an object
" of general attention, they wait very
" patiently for time to confute what was
" untrue in the report. Your extreme
" delicacy (for now that you are a little
" recovered I cannot help remarking
" that it is too exquisitely susceptible)
" and the peculiarity of your lord's dif-
" position make me see the consequences
" of this affair in a more serious light
                                    " than

" than I fhould otherwife do; but as I
" am afraid that neither of you will ever
" practife the philofophy which I fhould
" affume on this ridiculous occafion,
" I can only fay, that I fhall be ready to
" purfue any plan you fhall fuggeft for
" my conduct. Come, clear that pen-
" five brow; and be convinced, that
" Monteith may fee other men admire
" you without fuppofing that you en-
" courage their addreffes."

This fpeech had the defired effect.
It convinced the countefs that fhe
ought to conceal from her lord every
circumftance in her own behaviour
which excited the animadverfions of
others; and while her agitated fpirits
were fomewhat confoled by the hope
that his difpleafure was now wholly confined to Vernon, fhe faw the neceffity
of extreme caution, left it fhould ulti-
mately point at her. Her apprehenfions

fions of fome criminal intention in Fitzofborne's paffionate addrefs were tranfient. The extreme audacity and guilt
annexed to the bare idea of his having
formed an illicit attachment, and the
abfolute impoffibility of his even _hop-
ing_ for fuccefs, perfuaded her, that his
paffionate language was only, as he affirmed it to be, the unpremeditated fympathy of fincere friendfhip; and fhe now
blufhed at her own indelicacy in doubting, though but for a moment, the rectitude of his heart.

Efteem and confidence are never fo
powerful as at the moment of removed
fufpicion. She wanted an advifer and
confidant. Who could feem fo proper
to perform that office as the fagacious
fentimental Edward? The firft fcheme
which lady Monteith propofed to ftop
the circulation of the flanderous tale
was, that Fitzofborne fhould immediately

ately leave the family. The arch-tempter ſignified his perfeᴄt acquieſcence ; but with deference ſtated, that in his opinion ſuch an apparent coincidence with the prejudice of malevolence would tend to confirm its cenſure ; and to his repeated advice to treat the whole ſtory with indifference and bravado, lady Monteith oppoſed her own poignant feelings, which would never permit her to go into company while conſcious that a whiſper was circulated to her diſadvantage. At length a compromiſe was agreed to between the oppoſite opinions, and Geraldine determined to take leave of the gay world with more than philoſophic diſtaſte of its levity and uncharitable aſperity. Forgetting that retirement had ſometimes ſuggeſted the wiſh of introducing her brilliant talents to the noticeᶴof more accurate obſervers, the envy, hatred, and detraᴄtion which

impeded

impeded her career, made her again
wifh to take fhelter in the quiet undifputed fuperiority which Powerfcourt or
Monteith prefented. The prefence of
caprice and affectation renewed her Lucy's remembrance, rendered the recollected fweetnefs and ingenuoufnefs of her
character ftill more pleafing, and ftimu-
lated her impatience to pour her forrows into the bofom of foothing friendfhip; or to heal her corroded heart by
the gentle balm of parental tendernefs.
The propofed alliance which had occafioned her journey to London being to
all appearance entirely fruftrated, fhe
wifhed to return to the pleafing occupations of domeftic life; and the claims
of filial duty determined her to take
Powerfcourt in her way to Scotland.
To prevent any fufpicion, that her re-
treat was in confequence of a breach
between the earl and Fitzofborne, it
was

was propofed, that the latter fhould continue at Portland-place till lord Monteith's parliamentary engagements ter-
minated : and Geraldine entertained a
private hope, that her lord's intereft with
miniftry might procure fome poft which
would tend to reconcile Edward to the
fevere blow which his fortunes had received by the rejection of lady Arabella,
and at the fame time convince the world,
that caprice was not the diftinguifhing
characteriftic of all the Macdonald family.

Fitzofhorne now recurred to the converfation which had really been begun in
lady Fillagree's orangery; and he debated
the probable event of his renewing his
addreffes with fo much feeming anxiety,
and acted the part of the mortified fwain
with fo much adroitnefs, as entirely
removed every fhadow of fufpicion
from lady Monteith's mind, engaged
her

her anew in the office of a confoler, and even roufed a degree of felf-accufation at her having dared to fufpect that the morals of the virtuous Edward fell fhort of the perfection to which they pre-tended.   She lamented with pathetic fweetnefs the depraved ftate of female tafte, which gave a coxcomb infinite ad-vantage over a man of fenfe with the diffipated belles of the day; and Fitz-ofborne, refigning all his hopes of con-jugal felicity, with a profound figh de-clared, that in future he muft tranquillize his troubled foul with the endearing fympathy of female friendfhip.   He proceeded with platonic delicacy to draw the mental portrait of fuch a friend as he wifhed to find: carefully including in the enchanting compofition every grace which Geraldine feemed confci-ous of poffeffing.   Superior refinement, and an apprehenfivenefs of even juft

praife,

praife, was mentioned with emphafis;
and while the orator ftated the peculiar
difficulty in which this elevated fafti-
dioufnefs would place a fufceptible mind,
impelled by warm efteem to exprefs its
admiration, yet reftrained from fpeak-
ing by the certainty of offending, the
countefs liftened with unfufpecting delight : fo true is the maxim,

And while he tells her he hates flattery,
She fays fhe does fo, being then moft flatter'd.

Lord Monteith interrupted the converfation at a late hour. He returned
in very high fpirits, not only elated by
the triumph of his party, but with his
own particular fuccefs; having made a
neat and appropriate fpeech, confifting
of three or four well-turned periods,
which was honoured with profound attention. His lordfhip was lefs quick in
difcovering improprieties than in re-

14

fenting

fenting them when pointed out by others. Fitzofborne's fitting alone with his lady at five o'clock in the morning, alarmed him no more than Fitzofborne's efcorting her in a correfpondent drefs to lady Fillagree's fancy-ball. He recounted the events which had taken place in the debate with too much eagernefs to liften to the narrative of her adventures. He only heard with pleafure that Vernon paid no attention to her, and that fhe was perfectly in charity with her *cecifbeo*. So many agreeable occurrences made him readily confent to her propofal of paying her annual vifit to Caernarvonfhire immediately; and he was too fincere a friend not to enter with eagernefs into her plan of rendering Edward fome pecuniary fervices. His late difplay of oratorical ability feemed to enfure fuccefs; " for," faid he, " though I want nothing
" from

" from Government, why fhould not
" my friends reap fome advantage from
" the fatigue which I endure in the fer-
" vice of my country ?   Do you think
" that they dare refufe me, Geraldine,
" when they know how much I am
" courted by Oppofition?" He concluded by obferving, that Edward's talents
would do honour to any adminiftration.
His appearing in a confpicuous line
would alfo mortify Arabella, and convince her that fhe ought to have refpect-
ed her brother's *deeper* knowledge of
manners and characters, and not have
difmiffed a lover who was infinitely too
good for her.

CHAP. XXXI.

Meanwhile, by Pleasure's sophistry allur'd,
 From the bright sun and living breeze ye stray:
And, far in London's gloomy haunts immur'd,
 Brood o'er your fortune's, freedom's, health's decay;
O blind of choice, and to yourselves untrue!
 The young grove shoots, their bloom the fields
  renew,
The mansion asks its lord, the swains their friend;
 While he does riot's orgies haply share,
 Or tempt the gamester's dark destroying snare,
Or to some courtly shrine with lavish incense bend.
       AKENSIDE.

WHILE the earl of Monteith, with all
the blunt sincerity of his ardent character, pursued his friendly but unsuccessful design of serving Fitzosborne,
the polite circles were very merry at his
lordship's expence, every one wondering that he could not see what was so
extremely visible to every body else.

As lady Monteith had by retirement
fubdued the acrimony of competition,
even the candour of her rivals returned,
and the tide of popular opinion grew
ftill ftronger in her favour.   Large
allowances were made for a little vanity
and a little indifcretion. Moft people
fincerely believed that, after all, her
marked predilection for Fitzofborne
was nothing more than a harmlefs flirt-
ation, perhaps entered into out of frolic,
or with a view to mortify Arabella.
Thefe delicate extenuations were generally concluded by a laugh at his lordfhip's ftaying in town to vindicate her
character, and a fear, that fuch uncommon good-humour on his part might
encourage her to go greater lengths in
her *mirth* than fhe at firft intended.

The annihilation of domeftic happinefs
opening the faireft views for Fitzofborne's
fuccefs, he determined to employ every
engine

engine for its deftruction. The guarded
honour of Geraldine had hitherto re-
jected his infinuations to the difadvan-
tage of her lord with the warmth of
confirmed affection, and the indignation
which a confcioufnefs of the infeparable
union between his reputation and her
own muft infpire. But various inftances
had convinced him, that this "God
of her Idolatry" was vulnerable in a
thoufand points; eafily deceived, eafily
feduced, foon irritated, and as quickly
pacified. The prefence of the countefs,
her fuperior judgment, and the refpect
for the decencies of life, which his
ftrong attachment to her had infpired,
had hitherto preferved him from any
grofs acts of immorality, and given a
decorum to his conduct which juftified
the confidence fhe always placed in his
behaviour. Fitzofborne too plainly faw
that there was no innate principle to

preferve

preferve Monteith in the hour of temptation, when his guardian angel was abfent from her charge. Thofe temptations he refolved to fupply ; he doubted not his own ability to environ him with fnares, from which even a firmer virtue would find it difficult to efcape ; and yet at the fame time to conceal his infidious interference, and to cover his machinations with the proftituted names of friendfhip, fentiment, and morality. Though lady Monteith's enlarged underftanding had fufficient difcernment to difcover calumny; and to treat unfounded fufpicions with contempt, could fhe refift the evidence of truth ? or could her feeling heart fupport that cruel indifference which a diffipated hufband always affects to fhow to the amiable wife whom he injures by his vices ? Her ftrong fufceptibility at every circumftance which threatened the diminution

nution of their mutual regard convinced
him that fhe could not. And furely
the refentment which a young and beautiful woman muft feel at fuch injurious
negligence would render her an eafy
prey to the wiles of a feducer. To
fuppofe the contrary, was a paradox
which his knowledge of the human
character would not admit.

It is not my intention to pollute my
page by a defcription of thofe fuccefsful plans of iniquity by which Fitzofborne fubverted the principles of the
man who really loved him, and felt
anxious to render him effential fervices.
Unhappily, the world prefents too often
the fpectacle of one immortal being
alluring another to inebriety, or plung-
ing it in depravity, for me to excite
furprize by adding, that fuch actions
are not deemed incompatible with the
facred title of a friend. Thefe feducers
have

have not indeed always the deeper motives which I afcribe to Fitzofborne;
but let it be remembered, that the principles he profeffed gave a fanction to his
more monftrous atrocity.   Private vices
are public benefits.   Is it not a general
advantage, that property fhould be tranf-
ferred from an indolent fenfualift to an
active intelligent enterprifing citizen,
who would turn it to beneficial purpofes?
Monteith would be juft as happy with
his dogs and horfes, the only fphere of
enjoyment which his limited underftanding feemed capable of relifhing, though
his beautiful wife, and the fair poffeffions
with which fhe was endowed, were refigned to fome clever fellow who had
wit enough to acquire them.   Suppofing
the reftraint of confcience conveniently
filenced by that fcepticifm which is now
efteemed fo liberal, what other principle will you fubftitute to prevent fuch
practices ?

practices? Succefs foon reconciles the world to the profperous villain. A little declamation will fatisfy fentiment, and even the watchful dragon of honour may be charmed to fleep by honied words. Gratitude, which ufed to rank next to integrity in the fcale of virtues, is now, like its immediate predeceffor, degraded from its proud pre-eminence. Refinement has difcovered, that the giver beftows not from benevolent motives, nor from affection to the receiver, but merely to relieve himfelf from the pain of an uneafy emotion; and it has taught us to infer from thefe premifes, that it would be weaknefs to feel obligation for benefits which wholly proceed from the all-invigorating principle of felf-love.

Entangled in the mazes of an illicit amour, begun in a moment of inebriety, and purfued from want of cou-

rage

rage to be fingular, and want of energy
to be firm, the unhappy Monteith be-
held his prefent fituation with horror,
and contemplated his paft happinefs with
vain regret. His little daughters, his
Geraldine, his domeftic tranquillity, his
rural amufements,—how forcible was
the contraft between thofe guiltlefs pleafures, and the clamour of a Bacchana-
lian revel, the corroding inquietude of
a gaming-table, and the venal allurements of a courtezan.

Thoufand after thoufand vanifhed at
thefe midnight orgies. The image of his
injured wife and fupplicating infants conftantly rofe to his view; but they only
came to increafe his defperation, not to
reftrain his madnefs. The words, " One
" more bottle, and another fong! What
" Monteith a flincher? Come, my lord;
" luck muft change; make one more
" fpirited effort:" and, " Can the dear-
" eft

" eft of men, for whom I have refufed
" fuch liberal offers, defert me ?" Such
expreffions formed the magic fpells whofe
powerful incantations enthralled a mind,
reduced to the deplorable ftate of acting the part it abhorred, and adopting
the vices it defpifed, left the votaries of
diffipation fhould fufpect that he wanted
courage to be wicked.

Fitzofborne did not expofe his untainted reputation by *appearing* in thefe
fcenes of depravity. He contented
himfelf with pointing out parties which
he entreated his lordfhip to avoid, or
with mentioning inftances of furprifing
turns of luck at the gaming-table which
it would be folly in any one to expect.
He exclaimed againft Mrs. Harley's infamy, but acknowledged that fhe was
in the higheft fafhion ; that fhe had re-
jected a much larger fettlement than
what fhe now folicited from Monteith,

which

which he hoped his lordſhip would have
reſolution to refuſe; and yet, after all,
as the ſtrong bias of the paſſions ſeemed to point out that ſuch temporary
engagements were congenial to our na-
tures, their criminality muſt wholly depend upon the circumſcribed, and perhaps erroneous, ſyſtems of political ju-
riſprudence. He always concluded theſe
powerful diſſuaſions by urging the peculiar ſeverity of lady Monteith's principles, and the conſequent neceſſity of
concealing his miſconduct from her.
He conjured him to haſten to Powerſcourt; and then added, what he knew
would negative the propoſal, " How
" will you ſupport the tears and the re-
" proofs of that injured woman? For I
" fear, my friend, that in ſpite of every
" prudent precaution, your pale de-
" jected looks, embarraſſed manner, and
" conſtrained vivacity, cannot fail of
" attract-

" attracting her apprehensive observa-
" tion."

While the cruel machinations of Fitzosborne thus assailed the honour of Geraldine by vitiating the mind of her
husband, the destined victim of his worse
than murderous designs enjoyed the
soothing consolation of pouring her sor-
row into the attentive ear of friendship.
Ignorant of the severer trials which immediately awaited her, the tranquillity
of rural scenes, the benevolent simplicity of her revered father, the dignified
resignation of Mr. Evans, and the interesting sweetness of the amiable Lucy,
conspired to calm that painful conflict
which undeserved calumny and disap-
pointed hope had excited in her soul.
The early carol of the lark, the dying
fall of the nightingale, the kindling
glory of a summer's morning, the re-
viving freshness of the evening zephyr,

o 6 the

the various delights which the country
affords, and the attractive simplicity of
its uncontaminated inhabitants, infpired
lady Monteith with ftrong indignation
againft that faftidious tafte, which, while
it degrades the majeftic operations of
Nature with the epithets of ordinary
and vulgar, or paffes them with ftupid
infenfibility, purfues the celebrity required by the conftruction of a carriage
or the adjuftment of a robe. Her cenfures againft this petty ambition were,
however, too warm to be the dictates of
cool judgment, and evidently proved,
that the fair declaimer had been once
included in the frivolous groupe who
pay a blind idolatry to popular efteem.
Difappointment infpired other notions;
and, guided by this new impulfe, fhe
appeared once in her converfations with
Mifs Evans to lean to the dangerous
doctrines of Fitzofborne. " When I re-
" flect,"

" flect," said she, " on the evanescent
" nature of reputation; that it is acquired
" without solicitude, and lost without
" guilt; that it is the sport of calumny, and
" the battery from which envy mortally
" wounds the peace of innocence, I feel
" convinced that it is beneath the at-
" tention of a well-governed mind."

The conversation had been previously
confined to the caprices of fashion, and
Miss Evans was surprized that it should
produce such a serious conclusion; for
to this genuine child of Nature the eclat
annexed to the invention of a becoming
turban, or even the honour of an innu-
merable party, seemed unworthy of a
moment's anxiety. She therefore fixed
her intelligent eyes upon her friend, and
asked her to what she alluded in this
reflection?

" My own sad story," said Geraldine,
" is ever predominant in my mind.
            " Even

" Even while I am enjoying the de-
" lights of thefe beloved peaceful fcenes,
" I cannot for one moment forget that
" I am now a mark for public ridicule;
" and I am endeavouring to derive
" fome confolation from thofe fenti-
" ments which a gentleman, a very
" fenfible man, and a friend of lord
" Monteith's, has frequently fuggefted."

" They can only apply," faid Lucy,
" to the cafe of thofe who place their
" *ultimate* hopes in the applaufe of the
" world. They have nothing to do
" with the well-grounded mind, which,
" while it purfues the fteady path of
" duty, is pleafed with being encouraged
" on its journey by the modeft voice of
" well-earned praife. Far be it from
" me, my Geraldine, to feek to diminifh
" your confolations. Innocence allows
" you to poffefs a very fuperior one;
" and while your life difproves accufa-
                              " tions,

" tions, you have no caufe to be de-
" preffed.   Yet the watchful fufcepti-
" bility of female honour cannot but
" feel every attack upon its chara&ter;
" and it moft impatiently longs to refute
" the cenfures which its purity abhors.
" Lord Monteith's friend, I fuppofe,
" only made general obfervations.   He
" could not allude to your particular
" ftory."

" They were the obfervations of
" Fitzofborne," faid lady Monteith
gravely.

" Of Fitzofborne ?" interrogated
Lucy.   " I have heard you defcribe
" him as one of the moft enlightened,
" uncorrupted, and amiable of men :
" the perfon too, refpe&ting whom your
" condu& is cenfured."'

" It is exa&tly as you defcribe.   He
" is thus deferving, and I am fo ac-
" cufed."

" Does

" Does a fixed contempt for the good-
" will of that mafs of his fellow-crea-
" tures which is called the world, im-
" ply this fuperior merit? The world,
" I have heard my dear father often fay,
" judges right, but from wrong pre-
" mifes. It is hafty and rafh, not dif-
" paffionate and reflecting. It kindles
" into indignation at a fpecious tale: it
" loads a fufpected character with op-
" probrium; but however falfe its in-
" ference, however miftaken its judg-
" ment, its errors always lean to the
" fide of juftice and virtue. And I am
" the more inclined to pay a deference
" to my father's opinion, becaufe I find
" his idea of that aggregate body of
" which I am an individual confirmed
" by my own feelings."

" I fhall only join the general decifion
" of the world, which you fo reverence,"
replied the countefs, " when I found the
" praifes

" praises of Mr. Fitzofborne.   To the
" manners and the exterior of the moft
" finifhed gentleman, he adds the in-
" formation of the fcholar, and the pro-
" fundity of the philofopher.   Perhaps
" his ardent love of truth may urge him
" to too great a contempt for eftablifhed
" rules; and you know, Lucy, we muft
" not expect fuperior minds to pay a
" fcrupulous attention to the little
" punctilios which cuftom exacts from
" ordinary characters.   He is actuated
" by the moft exalted views, and his
" life is the nobleft comment upon his
" opinions."

The limited obfervation of Mifs
Evans had never difcovered fuch a
being as lady Monteith defcribed; and
fhe regarded the delineation of its diftinguifhed properties with fomewhat of
the fame kind of fcrupulous curiofity
with which we perufe the defcription of
the

the unicorn and the kraken; not abfolutely denying that fuch things may
exift, but wifhing to have their reality
more clearly identified. Her wifh was
foon gratified, and this human phœnix
was introduced at Powerfcourt by an
event in which chance (the modern
term for Providence) had a fmaller
fhare than *oftenfibly* appeared.

The poft always arrived at fir
William's in the afternoon: and though
the good baronet had nothing of the
bafhaw in his character, and was by no
means an adept in the fcience of politics,
he conftantly exercifed an unlimited authority over the newfpaper, the con-
tents of which he regularly recited, in
an audible voice, to the party affembled
round his hofpitable board. The journal
of paffing occurrences which found ad-
miffion at fir William's, was generally
uncontaminated by private flander, party
abufe,

abufe, or fulfome panegyric, and fimply
a plain narrative of the events of the day.
It *happened*, however, that after lady
Monteith had fpent about four months
at her father's, the following paragraph
found admittance :

    " It is rumoured in the polite circles,
" that a certain minifterial nobleman in
" the vicinity of P*******d Place, finds
" fufficient attractions in the beautiful
" Mrs. Harley to confole him for his
" recent difgrace; while a fair incon-
" ftant is trying, whether the keen air
" of the C**********fhire mountains
" may not be beneficial to a confump-
" tive reputation.   It is faid, that lord
" M*******'s fettlements on his new
" flame are uncommonly liberal."

    Sir William was not verfed in the
language of initials and afterifks; and
was not in poffeffion of the decyphering
gloffary which a knowledge of polite
                                  fcandal

fcandal fupplies.   After two or three
attempts to unravel the enigma, he delivered it to his daughter, with a requeft
that fhe would tell him what it meant.
A crimfon blufh and a dying palenefs
alternately took poffeffion of her face
while fhe perufed the paragraph. After
coolly obferving, that it was fome very
ill-natured nonfenfe, fhe complained of
faintnefs from the heat of the room, a
circumftance which her fituation, being
near her fourth confinement, might
render oppreffive. Mifs Evans's arm was
ready to lead her to her own apartment,
at the door of which fhe intreated her
friend to leave her, and to fuperintend
the backgammon party in her room, as
fhe much feared fhe fhould not be able
to rejoin them that evening.

No alarm was excited that night by
this circumftance.   Sir William's communications had been too confufed to
con-

convey any explanation to his auditors.
and any future appeal to the newfpaper
for information was impoffible, for it
had fuddenly difappeared during the
buftle occafioned by lady Monteith's
faintnefs. But fince the butler and the
houfekeeper were both very great poli-
ticians, and very anxious to infpect the
conduct of adminiftration, this circumftance too frequently happened to bear
at this time any myfterious air.

Geraldine's indifpofition wore next
morning a more ferious afpect. Her
maid owned, that fhe had been extremely reftlefs and agitated all night,
and her pulfe indicated confiderable
fever. Sir William's parental tendernefs took alarm. The moft eminent
medical affiftance which the country afforded was called in, and an exprefs was
difpatched to town to fummon her
hufband.

The

The petrifying power of vice requires time before it can render the heart completely callous. Lord Monteith had not yet forgot his inimitable Geraldine, the mother of his pretty little girls, the founder of James-town, and the benign enchantress whose magic powers had converted the wild unfrequented shores of Loch Lomond into the residence of plenty, elegance, and happiness. His recollection of the guiltless pleasures once enjoyed in her society aggravated his fears for her safety; nor could a thousand Mrs. Harley's detain him from her bedside. Endeavouring by the speed of his return to atone for the criminality of his absence, relays of horses were ordered upon the road, and the exertions of the postboys were stimulated by additional douceurs. But lord Monteith is not the only furious driver that has found it impossible to

7   travel

travel from himſelf.   New to the ſug-
geſtions of remorſe, yet unable to divert
the pain of its ſcorpion-ſting by the fallacious juſtification of comparing his
own conduct with that of other men of
faſhion, his troubled imagination continually placed before his eyes the
frightful image of an amiable wiſe mur-
dered by his vicious indifference ; and
his thoughts were alternately occupied
by curſing his own folly, and franticly
addreſſing Heaven to ſpare a life which
he now felt to be infinitely dearer than
his own.

Such a ſituation called for the ame-
liorating offices of friendſhip, and the
ſentimental, diſpaſſionate Fitzoſborne
had claimed that pious taſk.   To abate
the reader's indignation againſt that
gentleman's conduct, I muſt affirm,
that it was afterwards ſatisfactorily
proved, that the fatal paragraph which
I have quoted was not communicated

to

to the newspaper editor in a handwriting that bore the *leaſt* reſemblance to Edward's. I will alſo own, that his emotions during the journey to Powerſcourt were almoſt as poignantly diſtreſſing as thoſe of his fellow-traveller. Conſcience, indeed, was leſs loud in her accuſations, becauſe her ſenſibility had by frequent repreſſion been rendered more callous. But the probable diſappointment of thoſe plans of aggrandiſement which he had purſued with ſuch wicked diligence, haraſſed his apprehenſion; and he regretted, that human ſcience had not yet reached its ſummit of perfection, by preſenting to him the immortalizing elixir that would enable him to diſpute with death for the poſſeſſion of the victim whom he had marked for a more dreadful deſtination.

END OF THE SECOND VOLUME.

CPSIA information can be obtained
at www.ICGtesting.com
Printed in the USA
BVOW11s1547150817
492129BV00014BA/98/P